AF553093

ISLAMIC THEORY OF MOTIVATION

Insights from the Quran and *Sunnah*

ISLAMIC THEORY OF MOTIVATION

Insights from the Quran and *Sunnah*

DR. MOHAMMED GALIB HUSSAIN
Associate Professor and Head,
Department of Corporate Secretaryship, Islamiah College,
Vaniyambadi, Tamilnadu

and

DR. S.Y. ANVER SHERIFF
Associate Professor and Head,
Department of Commerce, C.A. Hakeem College,
Melvisharam, Tamilnadu

DEEP & DEEP PUBLICATIONS PVT. LTD.
F-159, Rajouri Garden, New Delhi-110027

ISLAMIC THEORY OF MOTIVATION
Insights from the Quran and *Sunnah*

ISBN 978-81-8450-296-1

Typeset by S.S. COMPOSERS
3190, Mohindra Park, Shakur Basti, Delhi-110034.

Printed in India at MAYUR ENTERPRISES
WZ Plot No. 3, Gujjar Market, Tihar Village, New Delhi-110018.

Published by DEEP & DEEP PUBLICATIONS PVT. LTD.
F-159, Rajouri Garden, New Delhi-110027.
Phones: 25435369, 25440916
E-mail: ddpbooks@yahoo.co.in • ddpubs@gmail.com
Showroom:
2/13, Ansari Road, Daryaganj, New Delhi-110002 • Telefax: 23245122

Dedicated to

Allah and Prophet Muhammad

(Peace be upon him)

for revealing us the knowledge

Contents

Preface

Motivation has attracted the attention of philosophers, psychologists, psycho-analysts, anthropologists and sociologists. Ever since Hawthorne experiments were conducted by Elton Mayo *et al.*, there have been attempts to fathom motivation in organisations. It is still continuous to be an elusive topic. Our ignorance of human motivation is far greater than our knowledge. Frederick Herzberg observed some thirty years back "what has been unravelled (about motivation) with any degree of assurance is small indeed." It is very much true even today.

Motivation theories originated in the west have underpinnings of Greek philosophy. They reflect the socio-philosophical thought of the times. The very fact that some of the old theories are discarded like worn out clothes and new theories are tried out exhibits the limitation of human knowledge. Human thought, however sound logically it may be, cannot be the only source of knowledge. Process theories of work motivation do not address the question of what motivates an employee. So-called content theories stop with describing self-actualizing nature of human being. Humanistic psychology goes a step farther, describes human motivation in terms of peak experiences and religious experiences.

Islam, one of the revealed religion for the mankind, answers the question what constitutes peak experience for human beings. It gives knowledge about the essence of divinity, creation, nature of phenomenal objects, life, life after death, man's role on this tiny planet. It provides answer to the question as to what is the essence of human being and his nature.

In every single human body resides, what the Quran

calls 'divine breath' or divinity. Man is partly spiritual and partly material. His body is made of matter. His soul (in the terminology of Islam, *Ruh*) is made of spirituality. Man has been sent to this planet to discharge the functions of vicegerent of God. Accordingly, he has been endowed with all the required faculties—his creativity, his productivity, his higher form of intelligence and his freedom and free will—to act on behalf of God. His role is described as *khilafat* (vicegerency). Though man has empirical ego (self) and given freedom by God to actualise this ego (self), man has inherent tendency to strive to please his Lord. He has innate nature of seeking pleasure of his Creator, Master, Nourisher and Sustainer. This inborn nature is: *will-to-raza-e-Ilahi* (seeking pleasure of divinity). Potentially, all human work or actions are directed to achieve *raza-e-llahi*. Work has propensity to stem from this inherent desire. Man by striving to seek the pleasure of his creator, actualises his self in the initial stages and then reaches a stage of *fana* (experimentally submerging man's ego in the Supreme Ego). He graduates to a mystical experience of *baqa* (subsisting in the submerged experience in His Lord all thorough his sojourn on this planet). This is experiential self-transcendence. This book articulates these experiences.

The authors express their sincere gratitude to the managements of Islamiah College, Vaniyambadi as well as C. Abdul Hakeem College, Melvisharam for providing moral and material support for embarking on this project. They are indebted to all the Secretaries and Correspondents—past and present—of these Colleges. Their thanks are due to Janab C. Khaiser Ahmed, Secretary and Correspondent, Islamiah College, Vaniyambadi and Janab S. Ziauddin Ahmed Chairman, The Melvisharam Educational Society, Melvisharam for their personal interest and patronage of the project.

The authors have been immensely benefited from the works of several writers in propounding this theory. To name all of them will be too much. Suffice it to say that in this theory building exercise, their views have impacted the thinking of the authors—consciously or subconsciously. In articulating the theory, the authors have been influenced and inspired by the lives of so many people. To all of them, the authors shall ever remain grateful.

Mr. G.S. Bhatia and his team at Deep and Deep Publications Pvt. Ltd. need to be congratulated for bringing out this book in a record time.

Valathoor

MOHAMMED GALIB HUSSAIN
S.Y. ANVER SHERIFF

1

Introduction

Human motivation, like a powerful magnet, has attracted psychologists, sociologists, anthropologists, psycho-analysts and management thinkers. Human behaviour is totally built on the motives and motivation of human beings. More so, it is the work-motivation that has fascinated the organizational behavioural scientists. The success or failure of any organization—business and non-business—squarely hinges *a priori* on the level of motivation of its members.

To help understand *raison d'etre* of what motivates a human being and what the process of motivation is, several western behavioural scientists have unleashed, in leaps and bounds, theories, propositions, prescriptions, ideas, concepts and models. These theories are now a part of the curriculum of the business schools, throughout the world. The basic contention of these principles is that they have universal application and validity, irrespective of socio-cultural milieu of the organizations. Western thinkers are of the firm opinion that this branch of knowledge holds mirror to its significances and practicality at all times to come.

The painstaking research carried out across the globe does not totally validate the concepts developed by western behavioural scientists. This shocking contradictory outcome even in the same culture, throws light on the fact that these theories have no universal validity.

The management practitioners, in business, industrial and service organizations are eager to understand what exactly the human nature is. They are rocked by the dilemma to what extent the remedies endorsed by the western behavioural scientists can be emulated for improving the motivational levels of their subordinates. They do harbour the doubt whether the human being is a self-actualizing creature. They are sceptic about the motives, so well articulated by western thinkers, such as need for achievement, need for self esteem, need for power, need for autonomy, etc.

The authors believe that any knowledge about a human being, more specifically, his or her motivational aspect should not be left to the plights of imagination of the human being, how creative it may be. Creativity of a theory does not vouchsafe its truth. The truth about human nature, about motives, about the process of motivation is to be obtained not from human thought, but from divine guidance.

An individual's vision, views, thoughts, ideas, concepts are conditioned by his/her personal experiences and his/her cultural moorings, etc.

Therefore, we have to search for the answer from divine guidance. The perfect divine guidance alone through light on human nature. The creator of the mankind alone knows well about the mankind, its motives and the process of improving the motives. This study is a modest beginning in that direction.

STATEMENT OF THE PROBLEM

The western theories of motivation that have been followed not only by the Muslim management practitioners but also by several others have proved to be ineffective, which necessitate the search for a universally applicable theory. The emergence of Islamic identity and revival of Muslim thought; the liberation of Muslim countries from the imperial western powers—both politically and intellectually—have necessitated the propounding of a theory based on Islamic prime sources.

The Islamic thought is very much compatible with the modern business organizations. It is more effective in solving management problems of today. The following are the factors that necessitate this study:

Blind transplantation of western models of motivation has proved to be null and void in many Muslim organizations as well as in other organizations.

The divine guidance about human nature has been lying in its sophisticated abstraction, but has not been articulated. Therefore, these abstract ideas about motivation need to be articulated.

The Western conceptualization of motivation gets rested with self-actualization on the part of a human being. The Islamic model of motivation rises the human being to a lofty level and even to the pinnacle of his real position.

The Western models of motivation—Maslow, Herzberg, McClelland *et al.*,—have reduced human beings as well as employees to the base level of need-gratifying animals. The gratification may be true in the case of animals but certainly not in the case of human beings who are created in the upright form.

It is needless to say that the business community, managers, academicians, behavioural scientists have no other outlet except to accept only that model which has a universal applicability and which is neither culture-specific, nor time-specific.

NEED FOR THEORY OF MOTIVATION

The employers do specifically lament about the lack of motivation on the part of their employees. They usually complain that they "pay their employees highest salaries, provide them the best possible fringe benefits, treat them with respect, but still they are not contributing the money's worth to the company." This is but the result of a wrong assumption about what motivates an employee. When a behavioural scientist suggests that money is the best incentive, the management provides the luring pay package to the employees. When an organizational theorist prescribes that the employees need to be given task autonomy, task significance, growth and advancement in the job and challenging work, the managements fall in line with such theorists. In spite of these concessions, neither the productivity nor the motivational level has come up to the expectations of the management.

One of the most frequently researched topics in organizational behaviour is motivation. One reason for the popularity of motivational research is that, the majority of employees do no exhibit enthusiasm towards their work.

As the traditional techniques of motivation have proved ineffective, there has emerged a dire need to draw on divine guidance for articulating a theory of motivation, which can be adopted not only by the Muslim organizations but also by the others. This study is a paradigmatic shift in the way in which individual as well as employee motivation is viewed. This paradigm is based on the Quran and the Sunnah which are given as the most fabulous gifts to the entire mankind—not only to Muslims—for all times to come. Therefore, the model developed here will command a universal applicability.

ISLAMIC CULTURE AND VALUE SYSTEM

The word, Islam, is derived from two Arabic root words: One SALM—meaning, 'peace' and the other SILM, meaning 'submission'. Islam means surrender of one's will to his Creator. Thereby, he is at peace with himself and also with His creation. In Islam, *sui generis* there is no demarcation between mundane and other worldly lives.

The word 'Culture' can be defined as shared values of a group of members. Islamic culture has the following instrumental and terminal values:

- Belief in the unity of Godhood (*Tawheed*).
- Belief in the institution of Prophethood.
- Belief in the different stages of human life.
- Belief in the ultimate aim of life to seek God's pleasure and through this, to attain salvation (*Falah*).
- Belief in man as vicegerent of Allah (*Khalifa*).
- Worship (*Ibada*).
- Knowledge (*Ilm*).

- Differentiation between Permissible (*Halal*) and Prohibited (*Haram*).
- Justice (*Adl*).
- No Tyranny (*Zulm*).
- Public Interest (*Istislah*).
- No wastage (*Dhiya*).

2

Methodology of Theory Building

One of the basic fallouts of renaissance in Western countries was the breaking of all shackles that binded human thinking. The religious scholars, priests and the church did not encourage or approve scientific research in 15th century. As a reaction of this dictatorial attitude of the church, the renaissance introduced Greek philosophy, logic, rational thinking and made man as the centre of the debate. Metaphysics, religion and philosophy were presumed to be unworthy of research. Unquestionably, this attitude had led to a scientific bent of mind and rationality. Anything other than a matter empirically investigated was rejected off-hand.

ISLAMIC CRITIQUE OF EMPIRICISM

Scientific investigation seeking knowledge through questions and answers, wonders associated with the creation of the universe, of the animals are very much accepted forms of research in Islam.

The very first revelation of the Holy Quran starts with the instruction to Prophet Mohammed (PBUH) to acquire knowledge.

Thus, spoke the Book of God:

> "Read in the name of the sustainer, who has created—created man out of a germ-cell! Read for your sustainer is the most bountiful one, who has taught (man) the use of the pen, taught man what he did not know."
>
> *(Quran 96: 1-5)*

> The Holy Quran has taught us to pray for knowledge: "O my Lord! Grant me increase in knowledge."
>
> *(Quran 20: 114)*

Prophet Mohammed (PBUH) had been reported to have said, "seek knowledge even it be in China." Islam divides education into 'Farze Ain' and 'Farze Kefaya'. Farze Ain is compulsory education which every Muslim is bound to pursue. It is this education that Prophet Mohammed (PBUH) had stressed. 'Farze Kefaya' is that learning which is acquired by some members and as a result one may get exemption from sin: viz. medicine, surgery, arithmetic, etc. Thus, Holy prophet had laid down that education should be made compulsory both for males and females, and that it should be sought even if it was available in such a distant land as China.

At different places in the Book of the Creator, human beings have been asked to brood upon the creation, the wonders of animals, natural phenomena, etc.

> "Verily! in the creation of the heavens and the earths; and in the coming and going of the day and night in alternation, there are indeed signs for men of understanding."
>
> *(Quran 3: 190)*

> "Those who remember Allah (always) standing or sitting or even lying down on their sides and think deeply about the creation of the heavens and the earth....."
>
> *(Quran 3: 190-191)*

Prophet Ebrahim (PBUH) went through the process of all the stages of scientific enquiry before he reached the conclusion that Allah was his Rub. The Holy Quran describes it beautifully in the following verses:

> "When the night covered him over, he saw a star: he said: 'This is my Lord'. But when it set, he said: 'I love not those that set'."
>
> *(Quran 6: 76)*
>
> "When he saw the moon rising in splendour, he said: 'This is my Lord'. But when the moon set, he said: 'Unless my Lord guide me, I shall surely be among those who go astray'."
>
> *(Quran 6: 77)*
>
> "When he saw the sun rising in splendour, he said: 'This is my Lord; this is the greatest (of all)'. But when the sun set, he said: 'O my people! I am indeed free from your (guilt) of giving partners to Allah."
>
> *(Quran 6: 78)*

Islam is not against scientific investigation but due to historical reasons, empiricism had gained undue importance in human life. Evidently, this was a reaction to religious persecution carried out in the Western countries. The biting tragedy of the mankind had been that at one time anything that opposed Christian dogmas was treated as blasphemy.

Islam maintains a right balance between empirical research and revealed knowledge. It encourages the scientific investigation that unravels the secrets of creation and the ideas for the betterment of human life on this planet. To say that anything beyond, scientific proof cannot be accepted into the body of knowledge depicts the biased attitude of western mind.

Revelation has to be accepted as the source of knowledge. In fact revelation is a boon of God to the humanity. When the first man, Adam (PBUH) was sent to the earth as the vicegerent of Allah, he was given specific knowledge by the Creator. The subsequent prophets were endowed with all effulgent divine guidance. This is what is called wahi-e-Ilahi [Revealed knowledge, Islam's basic contention is that as long as scientific findings do not go against the knowledge imparted by God, through different Prophets, it should be accepted as knowledge. The last message was sent to the mankind through Prophet Mohammed (SAW) in two forms: (a) the Holy Quran—immutable word of Allah, and (b) Hadith—the inspired sayings and doings of prophet Mohammed (SAW). Both are sources of revealed and *ad infinitum*. The basic difference between the two lies in their language. The Holy Quran is the word of God, and in the language of God. All the sayings and doings of Prophet Mohammed (PBUH) were also influenced by the indelible instructions of Allah. Almost through 23 years of life—the period of his prophethood—was under the direct control and guidance of Allah. What the Prophet did and he said, were all influenced by the divine instructions from Allah. The language was Prophet Mohammed's (PBUH). All knowing Allah occasionally relaxed His stiff but most essential control over the Prophet. The error that the Prophet committed in judging men and matters was immediately pointed out to him by Allah, to avert the repetition of such errors.

These two sources are accepted as the treasure boxes of knowledge for the entire mankind. There is a misconception among Western thinkers that, these messages of Islam are addressed to Muslims alone. The Quran addresses in several places as "O mankind." Islam claims that these two sources are relevant for all times to come. They were not the product of the culture prevailed during the period of Prophet Mohammed (PBUH).

It should be classified to limelight that when there is a conflict between empirical evidence and revelation, Islam accepts only the revelation and suffers no compunction in rejecting the empirical evidence, however scientific it may be.

As things stand by in social sciences, empiricism has failed in insurmountable amounts. They are mainly concerned in with the human behaviour. Following the pattern of investigation of sciences, such as Physics, Chemistry, Biology, Botany, etc. human behaviour has been thoroughly studied by the social scientists. Human behaviour in the realms of Economics, Psychology, and Sociology, cannot be reduced to the behaviour of Atoms, Protons, etc. The conclusions, based on empiricism are not universal. They are applicable to the societies in which the experiments have been carried out.

In management science, many of the conclusions had been derived from empirical studies that were carried out within certain groups selected on certain basics. Western empirical social science is based on the assumption that human behaviour is patterned and these regularities can be scientifically investigated and expressed as generalisations that reflect the universality of scientific law. But numerous studies have explained the social scientists' inevitable bias of the investigations. The psychologists and sociologists cannot get rid of their individual interests, values, culture and personal inclinations while studying the phenomena.

According to the German sociologist, Max Webber, total objectivity in social sciences is beyond human reach. Cultural values of social scientists do influence their theoretical propositions and their findings. The very fact that empirical investigation from different samples shows that the empirical investigation cannot be accepted as the only source of true knowledge.

Research in psychology, psycho-analysis and the social sciences examines the views and norms of human nature and social interaction, (which are incorporated into management theory) that are totally skewed towards western experience and the data has been drawn from western culture. This is the basic problem in psychological theories that have been developed in the modern West and specifically in the United States.

That is precisely the reason which has compelled the authors to embark upon a theory of motivation based upon divine guidance.

Islam is a complete system of life. Therefore, Islamic research cannot be restricted to any particular area. All the aspects of human life are covered by Islamic guidance. Any aspect of human life can be exemplarily examined by tapping the research methodology prescribed in Islam. The present research is an attempt to understand human motivation, in the light of the Creator's guidance.

Research, in the sense of seeking answers to intricate

issues and perplexing problems, is a legitimate Islamic activity. Many verses in the Quran begin with the word, "Yas-a-loonaka"—they ask you. A question followed by an apt answer is part of the Quranic way of bestowing knowledge. The knowledge of Quran has reached its beneficiaries from its flamboyant fountain—head, namely Allah Subhanahuwa Ta'ala, through angel Gabriel and Prophet Mohammed (PBUH).

The four bases of Islamic research methodology are:

- The Quran
- Ahadith
- Ijtihad (Discipline of fiqh refers to finding solutions, to problems, based on a specified methodology)
- Islamic Mysticism—Tasawuf

A. QURAN

The Quran Chef—d'oeuvre, is the final book of Allah to man. Allah Subhanawatalah has super numero attributes. One of them is the creation of the Book [KALAM] which is not subject to destruction. Therefore, the Holy Quran is indestructible and eternal. It was revealed to the final Prophet Mohammed [PBUH]. It was the pre-drafted book kept in Lohe Mahfoz. Allah's deep concern for mankinds welfare and well-being began revealing this book to Prophet Mohammed (SAW) who was accord prophet-hood at the age of 40. Allah (SWT) sent divine revelation to different Prophets, at different times. Notable among them are:

(a) Sahifa-e-Ebrahim,
(b) Torah,
(c) Zaboor, and
(d) the Bible.

The Quran drives home the necessity for the revelation because of the corruptions, interpolations and distortions that engulfed the followers of earlier Prophets.

The Torah was re-written entirely from memory after it was last for years and years. The message given to Jesus—

The Bible—was also distorted by his followers. The present Gospels of Máthew, Mark Luke and John [The New Testament] are not the writings, either of Christ or followers of Christ. The Gospels are the works of obscure authors at least a half a century after Jesus Christ. As against the previous revealed books, the Quran has been preserved in its pristine form.

This is a book which repeatedly asserts that it is no man's writing but a direct revelation of God. Endorsing its claim it challenges its readers to produce another writing of the sterling standard matching with the Quran if they exercise any doubt about its divine origin. The challenge is to bring out just three verses as splendid, as sanctified and as self-contended as the verses enshined in the Holy Quran. The challenge is yet to be answered even after fourteen hundred years.

B. HADITH

The sayings and doings of Prophet Mohammed (PBUH) and his silence implying a tacit disapproval of any act in his presence by his followers were all an inspiration from Allah. It was a different form of revelation. The Quran exhorts the people who believe the hadith of the Prophet as nothing short of the revelations.

> "And he does not speak out of low desires. It is not but inspiration which is inspired"
>
> *(Quran 53:3-4)*

The only difference between the Quran and the Hadith is that, the former was revealed directly through Gabriel, with every letter emanating from Allah; the latter was revealed without letters and words of Allah.

Hadith literature deals with several matters including theology, ethics and exegesis (explanation of the Quranic verses). The need for the explanation of the verses of the Quran arose quite early. Even before the whole Quran was revealed, people used to shower questing on the Prophet, or seek details on spiritual matters. The Prophet's answers were carefully preserved in the memory of his ardent companions

[ASHAB]. Those answers were written down. In the next generation, the Thabiun were those who were not personally with the Prophets. Subsequent generations established a chain of evidence through the Thabiun. And thus they paved a royal path for the growth of the science of Hadith. As the literature grew, it became necessary to establish rigid rules by which the evidence could be examined and confirmed. To activate and expedite the process of separation of the authentic traditions (SAHI) from those that were doubtful and worthy to be rejected (ZAIF), the science of Hadith was necessitated to be developed.

C. IJTIHAD-FIQH (JURISPRUDENCE)

The concept of reasoning in Islam is called Fiqh. When a new problem crops up, for which there is no specific answer in the Quran as well as in the Hadith, an attempt is made by the jurists to infer, with the Quran and the Hadith. This inference or reasoning is called Fiqh. An ocean of such literature has come up over the years on the basis of Ijtihad. There are four accepted schools of fiqh viz. Hanfi, Shaafi, Humbali and Maaliki. There is a group of Muslims who call themselves Ahle-Hadith, Salafi so on and so forth. They are not the blind followers of these four schools of fiqh. They have developed jurisprudence of their own.

However, there are basic differences in the concept of reasoning in Islam and reasoning in philosophy, especially the Greek philosophy. The European philosophers and the Greek philosophers tend to use abstract reasoning, a kind of rational analysis in order to build a philosophical system, which appears to be theoretically convincing. Never do they accept revelation as a source of knowledge.

In this study the Quran and the Hadith are used as the primary source. Any inference which is repugnant to these two primary sources is not consulted or accepted to form a part of this research.

D. ISLAMIC MYSTICISM—TASAWUF

There is a development of Islamic thought in the form of Tasawuf. On the intellectual side of Islam the science of KALAM, (built on formal logic) and the Ilm-al-Aquaid (the philosophical exposition of belief) have introduced elements on the spiritual side. Based on the intuition of the Mystic, Tawil (exposition of inner meaning of Quran and Hadith) has contributed a new dimension to Islamic thought. The Sufi Mystics adhered to the rules of their own orders. This study makes use of the Islamic Mysticism in formulating the Islamic theory of motivation.

3

Studies on Motivation

The prime objective of the study is to articulate a theory of motivation, which will have universal application and relevance in all times to come. Therefore, it is necessary to appraise and critically evaluate the existing theories of human as well as employee motivation. This chapter attempts to present a brief outline of various theories of motivation. An Islamic critique of these theories has been offered.

The concept of motivation can be traced back to western psychological works. Motivation has been defined by these authors in their own way depending upon the purpose of investigation. The *ipso facto* of these formulations is the human behaviour that is the goal targeted.

THEORIES OF MOTIVATION

Instinct Theory

Mc Dougall[1] states that the human mind has certain innate or inherited tendencies which are motive powers of all thought and action. These powers play a pivotal role in shaping the character and will of the individuals and in reshaping the destiny of nations. He defines instinct as "an inherited or innate psycho-physical disposition which determines its possessor to perceive, and to pay attention to objects of a certain class, to experience an emotional excitement of a particular quality upon perceiving such an object, and to act in regard to it in a particular manner, or at least to experience an impulse to such action."

According to Lawler,[2] Darwin was the first to call the attention of the scientific community to the possibility that much of human behaviour may be determined by instincts. Lawler points out that the instinct theory has been weakened as the list of these instincts has increased and has failed to predict the outcomes that the people have sought.

Drive Theory

According to Lawler,[3] the term 'drive' has been given precise theoretical meaning by Hull in his behaviour theory. The theory says that when a condition of biological need arises, drive would be produced and would activate the animal. These biological needs are the ultimate springs of action. The primary needs include the need for food, the need for water, the need for air and the need to avoid pain, the need to maintain optimum temperature, the need for sleep and so on. The drive strength can be increased by deprivation and it will be reduced as the need gets satisfied.

Lawler points out that the major shortcoming of this theory is its inability to explain motivation that is not based on primary drives.

Expectancy Theory

Toleman and Lewin through their research on animals and human beings had introduced terms such as expectations, valance and force in the 1930s. Toleman's work is concerned with purposive behaviour and congnitive expectations. Studies conducted by Toleman's showed that different types of goal objects were demanded with different strengths. If a change could be made in the reward system, it would induce a corresponding change in behaviour only after the new reward had a chance to be experienced.

Vroom[4] used the expectancy theory of Toleman and Lewin to explain work motivation. He assumes that a person has preferences among outcomes and calls these strengths of a person's urge for a particular outcome in relation to others as 'valance'. An outcome is positively valent when a person prefers it; it is zero when a person is indifferent and it is negative when he does not prefer it. According to Vroom, the strength of a person's desire or aversion for outcomes is not based on their intrinsic properties, but on the anticipated satisfaction or dissatisfaction associated with them.

'Expectancy' is defined as a belief that a particular act will be followed by a particular outcome. The Expectancy strength can be maximum or minimum depending on whether there is a certainty that the act will be followed by the outcome or not. In a model developed by Vroom, choices by persons among alternative courses of action were hypothesized to depend on the relative strength of forces. Each force in them was believed to be equal to the algebraic sum of the products of the valance and expectancies.

MASLOW'S THEORY OF NEED HIERARCHY

McGregor and others have used Maslow's[5] Need Priority Theory to understand job motivation. Briefly stated, this theory suggests that individuals do have a set of needs and they are arranged in a hierarchy shown below:

Physiological Needs

Need for food, clothing, shelter and sex.

Safety Needs

Need for protection against danger, threat and deprivation.

Social Needs

Need for belonging, association, for acceptance by the fellowmen, for giving and receiving friendship and love.

Ego Needs

They have been classified into two categories:

(a) *Self-esteem needs*—need for self-confidence, for independence, for achievement, for competition, for knowledge;

(b) *Regulation needs*—need for status, for recognition, for appreciation, and need for mutual respect.
(c) *Self-fulfilment needs*—need for realizing one's own potentialities, for continued self-development, and need for being creative.

The first three are classified as lower-order needs and the last two are categorised as higher-order needs. Maslow contends that the fulfilment of needs follows a hierarchy of their own. As one need is satisfactorily fulfilled, it is replaced by another. Maslow argues that man will think of satisfying his higher-order needs only after he gets satisfied with the lower-order needs. It is like running a race that has several destinations.

McCLELLAND'S THEORY OF MOTIVATION

McClelland[6] contends that many of the people can be classified into two broad groups. There is that minority which is challenged by opportunity and willing to work hard to achieve their objectives, and a majority which really are not achievement-oriented. Psychologists have tried to penetrate the mystery of motivation dichotomy. It is the need to achieve something (or absence of it) an accident? or is it hereditary or is it the result of environment? or is it a single, isolatable human motive or a combination of motives? or is there any technique that could inculcate achievement desire among those who do not have it now?

The studies made by many researchers, including McClelland, have provided partial answers and insights to most of the above questions. There is a specific human motive, distinguishable from others, which can be found and measured. This human motive, called achievement motive or "n Ach" (Need for Achievement) has several characteristics. Those who have "n Ach" prefer to work out a problem rather than leaving the outcome of it to chance or to others. McClelland admits that these individuals have a strong preference for work situation in which they get concrete feed-back on how well they are going. Why only a few people and not all think this way is a question of the hour. The evidence available to McClelland suggests that it is not because they are born that way, but because of special training they get at home from their parents who attain moderately high achievement goals but who are encouraging and non-authoritarian in helping their children reach their goals.

McGREGOR'S THEORY X AND THEORY Y

The propositions, Theory X and Theory Y, introduced by Douglas McGregor[7] in the late 1950's, described two opposing sets of assumptions that would appear to underlie the management practices. Theory X represents a series of propositions which are felt to be the conventional concept of the motivated.

Theory X managers assume that:

The management is responsible for organizing the elements of productive enterprise—money, materials, equipment, people in the interest of economic needs.

With respect to people, it implies a process of directing their efforts, motivating them, controlling their activities, and modifying their behaviour to suit the needs of the organization.

Without this active intervention by management, people would be passive or even irresistant to organizational needs. They must therefore be persuaded, rewarded, punished, and controlled. This is but the modus operation of the management.

The average man is by nature indolent, he likes to work as little as possible.

He lacks ambition; dislikes responsibility, and prefers to be led.

He is inherently self-centered and indifferent to organizational needs.

Man is, by nature resistant to change.

He is gullible and not very enthusiastic.

According to McGregor, the assumptions of this theory about motivation are inadequate. The "Carrot and Stick" theory of motivation which goes along with theory X is contrary to recent research findings in the field of motivation.

An alternative theory of management, proposed by

McGregor and known as Theory Y assumes that:

The management is responsible for organizing the elements of productive enterprises—money, materials, equipment, and people—in the interest of economic needs.

People are not by nature passive or resistant to organizational needs. They have become like that as a result of experience in organizations.

The motivation, the potential for development, the capacity for assuming responsibilities, the readiness to direct behaviour toward organizational goals are all the hallmarks of the workmanship of the employees. It is the responsibility of the management to make it possible for people to recognize and develop these human characteristics by themselves.

The prime task of the management is to arrange organizational conditions and methods of operation so that people can achieve their own goals best by drawing their own efforts towards organizational objectives.

To sum up the two theories, 'Theory X' places exclusive reliance upon external control of human behaviour, while 'Theory Y' relies heavily on self-control and self-direction. As has been pointed out by McGregor, this difference is the difference between treating people as children and treating them as mature adults.

LAWLER AND PORTER'S THEORY OF MOTIVATION

The theories that have been discussed so far assume that need satisfaction propels better performance. Lawler and Porter[8] contend that need-satisfaction does not result in better performance, on the contrary, performance leads to rewards—intrinsic and extrinsic—these in turn lead to satisfaction. Extrinsic rewards are those that are controlled by the management in the form of pay, promotion, security and so on. The relation between extrinsic rewards and performance is relatively unimpressive because of the difficulty of tying up these rewards with performance. On the other hand, intrinsic rewards are those which are given to the individual by himself. For example, it may be the joyful feeling of accomplishment of the task or any of the rewards that satisfy higher order needs of a person. They are more directly related to performance.

However, the relationship between rewards and performance is moderated by expected equitability of rewards. This refers to feelings of a worker as to what rewards he should receive in appreciation of his performance. Thus, satisfaction is the result of one's commitment to work and gaining rewards and replicas of recognition. In their study of job satisfaction of lower and middle managers, Lawler and Porter should support these managers in support of their theory.

INDIAN THEORY OF MOTIVATION

S.K. Chakraborthy[9] formulated the Theory of Motivation drawing examples from the Bhagwat Gita and the Vedas, which is known as the "Giving Theory of Motivation." The basic argument of this Thesis is that in India, people believe in sacrifice and they derive pleasure out of giving something or loving and caring for the other human beings. Therefore, this theory is superior to the Western theories of motivation.

ISLAMIC CRITIQUE OF WESTERN THEORIES OF MOTIVATION

McDougall states that the human mind has certain innate tendencies which are the motive powers of all activities. These powers are the basis from which the character and will of individuals and nations are developed. Islamic objection to this formulation is that it questions the source of these innate tendencies. The very fact that the instinct theory goes on adding to the list of these instincts, raises doubt about the finality of the theory.

According to the Drive Theory, when a condition of biological need arises, drive would get generated and activate the animal. And these needs are the spring boards of action. The primary needs include, need for food, water, air, need to avoid pain, the need for sleep, etc. The major handicap of this theory is its inability to explain human motivation that is not based on primary drives.

The Expectancy Theory of Motivation defines motivation as the algebraic sum of the products of the valance and expectancies. This theory is basically a process theory explaining the mechanical aspect of motivation. Since it is not a content theory, i.e. it dose not tell what precisely motivates a human being. The Islamic refutation of this theory is not essential.

The most celebrated of theories is the theory of motivation propounded as Maslow's theory of need hierarchy. This theory postulates that the individuals have a set of needs, and these needs are arranged in a hierarchical order.

As has been pointed out by Western behavioural scientists themselves that the need hierarchy postulated by Maslow fails to explain the entire human motivation.

This theory is basically a culture-specific. It is the product of American high thinking, developed about Americans and may hold good to few Americans.

This theory is a by-product of the western conceptualization of human being. In Western philosophy, the ultimate growth or pinnacle of growth of human endeavour is human-self. The votaries of this Philosophy cannot transcend beyond self-actualization. There is a world much beyond the self. The Islamic conceptualization transcends self-actualization of human nature.

McClelland has conceptualized need for achievement as the principle human motivation. However, the studies made by several researchers, including McClelland, have provided partial answers and insights to the question of need for achievement. This theory suffers from having no specific empirical support. The Western behavioural scientists themselves have criticized this theory on the following grounds:

This theory does not fully address the question of the process of motivation and how it really comes about. The very term achievement motive is not precise. Achievements can be induced temporarily. As already pointed out the evidence in support of this theory is fragmented and not conclusive.

The methodology adopted by McClelland is the famous

Thematic Appreciation Test (TAT) as the main tool. The main problem with projective technics as TAT is in its incorrect interpretation of responses.

The theory does not fully explain the process of motivation and its origin.

The two-factor theory of Fredrick Herzberg and his associates can be summarized thus: the determinants of satisfaction are qualitatively different from the determinants of job dissatisfaction. The presence of satisfiers catalyses the individual's job satisfaction, but the failure of these factors would not necessarily give rise to job dissatisfaction. This sort of dissatisfaction pains the employee and where there is pain, there cannot be pleasure. Joys and sorrows are not Juno's swans to go together. Presence of these factors will not result in pleasure.

The researcher agrees with some of the critics of this theory. The following is the gist of criticism of this theory:

Herzbergs theory is based on critical incident technic and therefore it is methodological specific.

The reliability of this theory is questioned. The interpretation of the data by the raters may contaminate the findings.

The theory provides only an explanation of job satisfaction and so it is definitely not a theory of motivation.

The motivation hygiene theory ignores situational variables.

The two factors are not really distinct, but both are the sources of motivation.

In addition to a number of other limitations, the most serious shortcoming of these Western theories is their pure materialistic orientation. All these theories share the assumption that man is basically a materialistic being and that he is primarily motivated by materialistic and temporal rewards. These theories ignore the actuality of spiritual, moral or metaphysical dimensions of human motivation. In view of these serious shortcomings, the Western or modern theories of motivation tend to be uni-dimensional, imbalanced and rather inadequate.

The Western models conceive organizational motivation, as human relationship building tool between the organizational member (the employee) and the organization (particularly organizational leaders). An important aspect of this relationship is that the organization or its leadership is seen to be the source of motivation for the employee.

The Islamic perspective perceives organizational motivation as a human relationship, but one that springs from or is anchored in the relationship between the individual and God or the Creator or Allah. This implies that the cornerstone of employee motivation is not the individual's instinctive needs but his relationship with God—which has a purpose, i.e., seeking or attaining the pleasure of God or the Creator.

Notes and References

1. Mc Dougall, William, 1918, "An Introduction to Social Psychology", Boston: John W. Luce and Co.
2. Lawler, E.E., 1973, "Motivation in Work Organizations", Monterg, Call Brooks Cole Publishing Co.
3. Lawler E.E. and Porter, L.W., 1976, "The Effect of Performance on Job Satisfaction", London: The Macmillan Press Ltd.
4. Vroom, V.H., 1964, "Work and Motivation", New York: John Wiley and Sons.
5. Maslow A.H., 1954, "Motivation and Personality", New York: Harper.
6. Mc Clellend, D.C., 1969, "That Urge to Achieve Readings in Management", Ohio: South Western Publishing Company.
7. Mc Gregor, D., 1960, "The Human Side of Enterprise", Tata McGraw Hill Publishing Co., Ltd.
8. Porter, L.W., 1961, "A Study of Perceived Need Satisfaction in Bottom and Middle Management Jobs", *Journal of Applied Psychology*, 45(1).
9. Chakraborthy, S.K., 1980, "Management Stylistics in India", The case for a countervailing Ethos, *Decision*, July 1980.

4

Islamic Theory of Motivation

The mind boggling question that has baffled the philosophers and psychologists down the ages is what the motives are that propel a human being to do certain acts. There are innumerable motives that trigger action and in abstract form, they can be divided into the following categories: needs, desires, sexual drives, passions, divine soul (Rooh-e-malquti), etc.

Needs are those drives which are necessary for the preservation of human life. Need for hunger, need for thirst, need for protection of body and need for protection from enemies, etc. are some of the needs that warrant an immediate and fruit-bearing activity.

Desires or wants are a step far ahead of needs. When a person feels hungry his is a need for hunger. This can be satisfied with an ordinary meal. It becomes a desire if he wants a specific type of food. Thirst is a need. It can be quenched by taking plain water. It becomes a desire, if the individual prefers to quench his thirst with a soft drink.

* In articulating this theory, the authors have been influenced by numerous Islamic theological and mystical treatises. The authors wish to express his sincere gratitude to all the authors of these works. Since the theory formulation is the attempt of the authors no citations are given except the Quran and Hadith.

Need to protect one's body can be satisfied by putting on the required clothes suited to the climate. However, it becomes a desire if one goes for expensive or stylish dress. Need for shelter can be fulfilled by having an ordinary house. If he constructs a palatial building, the need graduates into a want. Similarly, status, fame, power, etc. are wants and not needs.

Sexual drive can be considered as a need. However, the researcher is of the opinion that this gets manifested and plays a vital role in human life and therefore, it is treated as a separate motive. Sexual urge plays a vital role in today's advertising, arts, literature, culture but there are several branches of human life in which sexual drive does not play a vital role.

Passions such as love, affection, hate, care, revenge, jealousy, etc. are some of the emotions, embedded, in human life. Their manifestations occur at a higher plane. They have their say in arousing human emotions. Unless they are checked and controlled, they may lead to the annihilation of human species. They are harmful like the pointed edge of the sword. One desire leads to several other passions like the saying "one evil leads to several other evils."

The above four motivational forces and their motivational basis have been beautifully described in the following verse of Holy Quran:

> "Man is thrilled in persuit of enjoyment in women, children and accumulated riches, heaps of gold and silver, and horses marked of selection, cattle and well-tilled land; but there are contemptible things for the life in the world of this side end; whereas there are much better than those things, and an excellent status, with Allah, in the life of that side end."
>
> *(Quran 3: 14)*

The fifth motivational force of a human being is his divine spark. This is also called Rooh-e-malaquti. Allah has gifted all human beings with this blessing. The Holy Quran puts it in a catchy way:

> "Then when I have formed him and breathed into him of My spirit, fall down unto him prostrate."
>
> *(Quran 15: 29)*

It is this divine spark, the golden speck of divinity which has made the human beings the best of creatures. (Ashraful Maklukath). Angels were asked to bow before this divine spark. It is because of this a human being has got the innate ability to demark good from evil. He was endowed with the ability to adopt and practice humanistic values. Since he is gifted by the heavens, he has a burning desire to move towards divine guidance. He has the inner potentiality to turn always towards his Creator. This is what distinctly distinguishes a human being from animals. It is this light that makes a human being receive the revelation from his Creator. This is the divine motivation, which propels a human being to embark upon finer and fetching activities. It is this divine spark, which makes him repent for the sins committed; for the evil desires, nourished, for the passions nurtured and for the ambitions harboured. It is this divine spark, which galvanizes him to do any act to seek the pleasure of his Creator. In this chapter an attempt has been made to articulate this peculiar aspect of divine spark and its ramifications to motivate.

CREATION-TRANSCENDENCE

The creation verse (Ayat-e-Taqliq) enlightens about the creation of objects:

> "Verily, His command, when He intends a thing, is only that He says unto it, "Be!" and it is !"
>
> *(Quran 37: 82)*

In the above verse we find the word "thing" refers not only to all the objects in the Universe but also to human "self." Hence it is clear that Allah is addressing all things and the command is "Be." These things include the things that are existing and those that will be created. It is necessary that the thing, which the Divine will, desires to bring into existence externally and which is the object of its address should subsist in Allah's Mind and should be non-existent externally.

The following lines throw more light on this:

> "He said, "Even so (it will be, in the existing circumstances) your Lord says: 'it is to Me easy. Surely, I have created you before, when you had been nothing."
>
> *(Quran 19: 9)*

The object is known to Allah, before its creation. It subsists in the mind of Allah. Evidently, the Creator must possess knowledge of His creatures prior to creating them. A further proof of His astounding is described knowledge in the following verses:

> "Should He know not what He created? And He is the one that understands the finest mysteries and is well acquainted with them"
>
> *(Quran 67: 14)*

> "Is not He, who created the heavens and the earth, able to create the like of them? Yes (indeed) He is the All-knowing, Supreme Creator."
>
> *(Q: 36: 81)*

> "He will give them life, who created them for the fist time! For He is Knower of every creation."
>
> *(Quran 36: 79)*

The Holy Quran is making it explicit by the above verses, that all the things have taken their shape and from out of the ideas of Allah.

> Everything, externally is, a creature, Allah is its Creator—"Allah is the Creator of everything."
>
> *(Quran 7: 54)*

The essence of things before creation subsists in the divine knowledge. They are the objects of God's knowledge;

they are the "Ideas of Allah; these are the objects of His command. They have an innate ability for emerging from the inward into the outward. At the word of command of Allah, they make their appearance and are termed creatures. The whole world for its internal as well as external existence depends upon Allah. The world of things owes its existence to Allah, because things are the brain children of the Divine Self. They borrow their existence and importance from Allah. They were in void of external existence before their creation.

The nature of relationship between the Creator and the creatures is something like the Knower and the known. This relationship is not one of identity but it is surely that of otherness. There exists the relationship of otherness between the essence (Zath) of the Creator and the essences of His creatures.

A painter conceives the idea of a garden; he then transplants it on the canvas. The garden exists as an idea in his mind. It depends for its mental existence totally in his mind. And his mind is the soft and sweet bed of the idea. Any idea is a form that is, and it as its own determination which has his own boundaries. On the contrary, the painter's mind has no such limitations. The knower and the known, the mind and the mental image are by no means identical. The painter is not the painting, neither the painting the painter. They are totally different from one another like the sea and the sky. Similarly. it could be said that a relationship of otherness is found between the essence of Allah and the essence of things. Allah, being a Knower, from eternity is aware of His own thoughts. These ideas of Allah are called latent realities (Alayan-al-Thabita). When they are manifested, they become created things (Khalq).

Even as ideas, things are not identical with the essence of Allah. The basic differences between Allah, the Knower and the ideas of God or essences of things are listed out below:

THE KNOWER	THE KNOWN
• He is free from any limitations—has no form	• Has a form, having limitation or individualization

• Exists in himself depending on nothing else but Himself	• Subjects in the mind of the known; does not posses its own independent existence
• Possesses positive attributes: for e.g. Life, knowledge, willpower, hearing, sight and speech	• Possesses no attributes like knowledge, or will unless given
• Is active	• Is passive, having no existence

From the above tables it is clear that the relation between the known and the knower is one of otherness, never of identity. The essences of things are the ideas of God and are co-eternal with God. Allah is one and His ideas are plenty. Allah exists independently but ideas depend on the mind of Allah for their existence. The essence of Allah is free from any limitations; the ideas are determined in form, possessing their own characteristics named as 'Shaklaat' in the Holy Quran.

If the ideas are the others of God; things, which are the external manifestations of ideas, must also be others of God. Allah has manifested externally, in the essence of things. The essence of Allah, the Exalted, does not resemble that of any of His creatures, as verified in the verse, which reads,

> "There is none like unto Him and He is the hearer, the seer."
>
> *Q: 42: 11)*

> Yet another seraphic description of Him is, "He is the one, the soul, the indivisible."
>
> *Quran 112: 1-2)*

Basically things are different from Allah. This difference is not nearly suppositional but is the difference of essence. He is transcendent in the sense of being self-begotten, self-caused and self-existence. He is unmovable and beyond all abstractions and inferences.

The relation between Allah, the One the Transcendent

being (not in the likeness of anything) to many things in the universe may be meaningfully illustrated in the following theological language:

THE ONE	THE MANY
• Khaliq (Creator)	• Makhluq (creatures)
• Rubb (Lord)	• Marbub (slaves)
• Ilaa (The worshipped)	• Maluh (worshippers)
• Malik (Master)	• Mumluk (servants)

Thus, the gist of the whole doctrine, tabulated above, is that no man can become Allah.

The same idea is beautifully poeticized in the following lines:

The Abd (worshipper) will remain Abd
Whatever the progress he might make
The Lord will remain the Lord
However low He may descend
And the transfer of essence is impossible.

Therefore, Haq (reality) is Haq and the Abd is Abd, like the saying, 'Verismo is Verismo'.

Such discussion takes us to the first part of the article of faith expected in a Muslim. "There is none worthy of worship except Allah and Mohammed (PBUH) is His Prophet. The word, La (none) negates divinity from idols (The essence of contingent beings), negates Lordship and negates attributes and existence.

IMMANENCE

It is a hundred dollar question that how these aspects of Allah are related to all other created beings and how limitation is caused in them.

The Quran asserts that Allah is immanent in all beings. This immanence is revealed in a multifarious forms and ways supernumero.

> "And He is with you wheresoever you may be. And Allah is All-seer of what you do."
>
> *(Quran 57: 4)*

The word, "wheresoever", generalizes the place and the phrase, "you may be" generalizes time.

Allah discloses in the Holy Quran.

> "They are experts in hiding their disposition from people; but they can never hide their disposition from Allah; for He is present with them even when, by night they devise secret plans together against Allah's will. Allah has encompassed all that they do."
>
> *(Quran 4: 108)*

This sacred verse testifies Allah's gracious presence with us. The words used are: compass them round (Muhit). Allah is all around us and Allah knows all about us. Therefore, His presence with us is indisputable. In one of the Hadiths the Prophet Mohammed (PBUH) said: "Any one of you while offering prayers, should not spit in front of himself, as Allah is before him." This Hadith, has prompted the theologists to argue that the omnipresence of Allah is obvious. This Hadith refutes the idea of Allah confining Himself only to Arsh (Throne).

> Allah is near us. The Holy Quran says: "We are nearer to him than you, but you (can) not see."
>
> *(Quran 56: 85)*

The pronoun, We, (Nahnu), in the above said verse is 'Zath' and by linking with the simple conjunction 'but', the possibility of attribute to nearness is dispensed with. Personal nearness is stressed and Allah, in this verse does not say "you do not understand." He only says, you do not see. He expresses His nearness to His ardent Votaries:

> "And when my servants ask you, how to get nearness of Me (enlighten them) "I am very close to all who invoke Me (only), and respond to every supplication

> made to Me (without any mediator); hence they should obey Me; and believe in Me, so that they may be led aright."
>
> *(Quran 2: 186)*

In another verse Allah describes his nearness to man,

> "We are nearer to him than his jugular vein."
>
> *(Quran 50: 16)*

Allah knows the innermost motives of man even better than man does himself know. He is nearer to a man than the man's own Jugular vein. The jugular vein is the big trunk-vein, one on each side of the neck, which brings the blood back from the head to the heart. The two jugular veins correspond to the two arteries, which carry blood from the heart to the head.

All the above verses do reflect the personal nearness of Allah and not the one gained through knowledge.

The following Hadith still identifies the personal proximity of Allah: Abu Moosa Ashari said that once he accompanied the Prophet together with others on one of his journeys. His companions (Sahaba) started saying:

> "Allah is great" very loudly. On hearing it, the Prophet said, "O. people, do not be too hard on your ownselves (say it gently). You are not addressing any unseen or deaf, you are calling the Being Who is listening to you, seeing you and who is with you. The one whom you are addressing is near to you than the neck of your camel."
>
> *(Muslim, Bukhari)*

Allah encompasses all things. The Holy Quran says:

> "And to Allah belongs all that is in the heavens and all that is in the earth. And Allah is Ever Encompassing all things."
>
> *(Quran 4: 126)*

In another verse it is pointed out: "Unquestionably, He it is who is surrounding all things!"

(Quran 42: 54)

While answering the questions lavished by the Jews, Hazrath Ali had remarked,

"God is glorious. He is superior to the concept of one who says that our God is space bound. He does not know his Lord and Creator. Verily, Allah encompasses every space."

Allah is omnipresent. The Hoiy Quran says:

"The east and west (and) all (the directions) belong to Allah; so wherever you turn your face, you would find sanction from Allah. Indeed, Allah is most generous, all-knowing."

(Quran 2: 115)

As Allah encompasses all things so he is present in his essence in everything. Wherever you turn your face, whatever thing you find, Allah's essence will be found in them.

Allah witnesses all things by Shahid,

"Verily, Allah is witness over everything."

(Quran 22: 17)

Allah is present and cannot disappear. Allah is a proper name and witnessing in His attributes and an attribute can never be separated from the essence. Allah is present with everything.

To quote one more verse,

"In whatever disposition you may be and whatever portion you may be reciting from the Quran, and whatever deed you may be doing, We are witness there at and you are under constant observation of Us. And nothing is hidden from your Lord so much as the weight of an atom on the earth or in the heavens, not

> less than that, nor greater, but it is entered into a clear Record."
>
> *(Quran10: 61)*

The manifestations such as the "Firstness", the "Lastness", "Outwardness" and "Inwardness" of Allah are well brought home in these lines:

> "He is the First and the Last, the Evident and the Hidden; and He has full knowledge of all things."
>
> *(Quran 57: 3)*

The pronoūn, in the above verse He refers to essence (Zath) of Allah. And all these four terms are definitive in character. In all the four aspects of existence, Allah's being alone is posited. And the existence of any other being, other than Allah is negated.

The beautiful commentary of the above verse can be found in the prayer of Prophet Mohammed (PBUH),

> "You are the first, so there was nothing before you; and you are the last, so there is nothing after you; and you are evident, so there is nothing above you; and you are the inward and there is nothing below you."

Allah alone is the first and there is nothing before Him. He alone is the Last and there is nothing after Him. Thus, the existence of things has been negated from the last aspect. Allah alone is outward, there is nothing above Him. When Allah alone is the First and the Last and the outward, then He alone would be the inward too. That is why, the Prophet stated:

> "you alone are inward and there is nothing below him."
>
> *(Quran 57: 3)*

In the above verse; the First and the Last, could be explained with the support of another authentic Hadith known as 'Hadith-e-Dlaw'. It proves the immanence of Allah.

A part of the Hadith reads, "If you; let the rope descend to the lowest depth of the earth, even there it will assuredly touch Allah." Then the Prophet quoted the above verse

It is stated in the Hadith quoted by Tirmizi and Abu Dawood, that the Prophet after counting upto divine Throne, accepted "There is Allah above this."

After giving the knowledge of what is above the throne ("Arsh"), the information regarding the lower region was also necessitated. In the Hadith-e-Dlaw he turned his attention from the higher to the lower region, i.e. from the first to the last. After describing the distance of all the seven layers of the earth, the Prophet (PBUH) said that there is Allah even in the lowest region too.

According to another verse,

> "And He is Allah in the heavens and on earth."
>
> *(Quran 6: 13)*

the same Allah manifests Himself in heaven and earth, severely in all His glory.

And thus, existence belongs to Allah alone. The attributes and the actions are peculiar to Him.

SECRACY OF CREATION

The baffling question is that how the essence of things which is but the idea of God has derived its existence. Equally, puzzling is yet and for question and it is about the mystery imbedded in the command 'Be' and "it is."

Ideas are the accidents of some substance, which is the absolute being alone. The following verse substantiates what has been described earlier:

> "He has created the Heavens and the earth from Haqq."
>
> *Quran 6:3)*

In another verse, Allah emphasizes the same:

> "Allah created the heavens and the earth from Haqq.

But most of them do not understand."

(Quran 44: 39).

According to Shariat and the lexical definition, Haqq alone is the word to denote the absolute being. Etimologically, haqq is derived from the word 'haqiqat' (reality). All the ideas or the essences of things are derived from haqq and are manifested in haqq. Therefore, the essence (ZATH) of Allah and His existence are at work in the creation of the world. This is the secret of the saying, "He is the outward." The Verse:

"Allah is the light of the heavens and the earth."

(Quran 24: 35)

Further adds strength to this statement. The essence of Allah which is absolute existence, by virtue of its manifestation is called Noor (light). And light is that, which is visible in itself and makes other things visible.

Allah in His own immutable state, being without altering His individuality manifests Himself through his "Noor" in the form of phenomenal objects. These objects are reflected entities expressing outwardly the essences which subsist in the knowledge of God. Thus the divine aspects (being attributes, etc.) have come to be associated with the world of creation.

The things that are created have not have been created out of nothing, because out of nothing, nothing can be created. Nor does it mean that the absolute manifests itself in the form of things. Allah cannot be divided into parts, because He is above all the limitations and individualization. Allah manifests Himself in the form of phenomenal objects. This manifestation takes place in accordance with those ideas, which are latent in God and subsist in His knowledge. It is as a result of this manifestation that phenomenal objects take their shape depending on their merit and capacities.

Tajalli or self-manifestation is supported by Quran and Hadith. The researcher provides an illustration on Tajalli. Suppose we bring to our mind a picture of our dear friend, who is taking an evening walk with his wife and children. As soon as we think of him, our mind assumes the form of our friend and presents his family picture before us. But inspite of this manifestation, despite their multiplicity, our mind is just one.

After understanding Tajalli (manifestation) we should realize, how Allah maintains His immutability without change and multiplicity. Allah manifests Himself in his thought forms through the attribute of Noor (light). The manifold varieties of ideas and their determinations cannot make any difference in the personal unity of God and His transcendence.

The word, Tajalla, is seen in the Quran as depicted in the following verse:

> "...............when his Lord manifested (Tajalli) his glory on the mount He made it as dust, and Moses fell down in a swoon."
>
> *(Quran 7: 143)*

Allah manifested Himself before Moses on Mount Sinai through a tree, in the form of light and fire.

> "But when He revealed it, he was called from the right side of the Valley in the blessed field, from the tree: O, Moses! I, even I, am Allah, the Lord of the worlds."
>
> *(Quran 28: 30)*

The Hadith of Prophet Mohammed (PBUH) provides support to the above contention. In the tradition cited from Abu Sayeed Qudri (RAL), which is known as Hadith Tahavvul, is given that during the day of judgment Allah will reveal Himself to every group, in the form of its deities:

> "On the day of judgment, the announcer will ask loudly every group to follow whom they worship. All those who worshipped deities other than Allah, having a shape or not having a shape, such as stone, wood, etc., will find their way into hell and worship their deities there. Now, they will leave those pious persons and sinners who worshipped Allah alone. The Lord of the worlds will come to them and say, "Whom you are

waiting for, every group has followed its own deities?" And they will reply, "O, Lord, we had disassociated ourselves from these people in the world itself. This is our ultimate goal that when our Lord comes to us we will recognize him. Allah will ask them "Have you any method by which you can recognize Him?" They will say, "Yes, we do have."

All glorious Allah will make His dazzling appearance through "Saq" (comparative attribute). "Allah can never manifest Himself without a form, manifestation is always possible in forms and modes only"

The fact is supported by a Hadith of Tibrani and Hakeem. "The Lord will appear before them in assumed forms."

In the Hadith quoted by Abu Musa Ashari it is recorded, "He will come out in His glory smilingly." Huzaifa, in another Hadith, quotes the Prophet "He will appear before them and cover them in His light."

In another Hadith about the vision in Miraj, Tirmizi has quoted from Ibn-Abbas "Allah appeared in the glow of His own light and the Prophet beheld Him twice. The prophet beheld Allah in wakefulness in a definite form."

According to Shariat, Allah's assumption of forms is an accepted reality. But this assuming of forms does not conflict with His essential transcendence. Gabriel used to appear before Prophet Mohammed (SAW) in different forms, but such an appearance did not change the nature of the angel.

Allah possesses both attributes of 'inwardness' and 'outwardness'. The inward rank is of absolute transcendence (Tanzih Mutlaq), it is the divine essence unknown and unknowable, absolute, unseen and immanence. In the Holy Quran, both transcendence and immanence verses are found in plenty. To believe in one and reject the other is not the right form of faith. The perfection of Muslim faith depends upon belief. Allah is immanent. He comprises both immanence and transcendence. The right way would be to believe that Allah is immanent in His transcendence. He is manifest with His own purity and transcendence in the likeness of everything.

TANAZZULAT (THE DESCENT OF THE ABSOLUTE)

The above conceptualisation informs us that the created and the Creator are both real, though different in their essence. One was real in its essence while the other was real as the reflection of the other. The created things are real as far as they reflect the reality of the infinite. They are real, more or less, in proportion to the clearness of the reflection of the reality of the Creator. Thus, reality itself has been classified. The grade of reflection determines the reality of each created thing. The diversity existed and played a pivotal role in the universe. All the things that are created have uniform nature as far as they all reflect the same ultimate reality of the Creator. This classification of reality is called Tanazzulat.

In the following pages, an attempt has been made to delineate various aspects of Tanazzulat. This is also called the theory of Tanazzulat-e-sitta. Allah is an absolute being. He has no partner, no equal. Neither His opposite nor His like exists. He possesses neither form nor shape. Neither He has an origin nor an end; He is free from all limitations. According to the Quran, "He is not in the likeness of anything." He is free from all the aspects of the created beings.

The human senses, thoughts, reasons and understanding are at a loss to find Him. Admission of inability to pursue is itself a sort of perception.

The same Haqq (absolute being) reveals Himself in different forms or descends in these forms. The stages of descend are innumerable, but the most marked of these are six. These are termed the six descends, (Tanazzalul-e-sitta). The first three of them are called Maratib-i-ilahi (divine ranks) which are called Ahadiyat (Abstract oneness), i.e. the state of the essence, the colourless, infinite, the indeterminate. The second is Wahdat (unity) and the third is Wahidiyat (unity in plurality). The remaining three are called Maratib-i-kawni (worldly ranks), which are Rooh (spirit), Mithal (similitude) and Jism (body). Man comes last of all these and his rank is inclusive of all other ranks. The following table will explain some of the technical terms and the order of states:

This table is reproduced from Moulana Asharaf Ali Thanvi's book Kitabul Takashuf:

TABLE

First plane zath state of essence	*Second plane first descent*	*Third plane second descent*	*Fourth plane third descent*	*Fifth plane fourth descent*	*Sixth plane fifth descent*	*Seventh plane sixth descent*
Ahadiyyat state of unity inward	Wahdat	Wahidiyat	Rooh	Mitnal	Jism	Man

A brief explanation about some of the points given in the table are discussed below:

1. Ahadiyyat

It is the state of an abstract unit. Ahadiyyat implies the absolute being of Allah. This being, according to its essential nature, is unknown and unknowable. He is spoken as the "Absolute "Ghayb"—the unseen. The essence of Allah means the absolute dropping of all modes, relations, and aspects. This absolute being is the pure essence in which there is no manifestation, no name, no quality, no relation or anything else. So, when anything else is manifested in it, that manifestation is ascribed not to the pure essence but to which is manifested. The essence, in the requirement of its own nature, comprises particulars, relations and adjuncts. The requirement of their disappearance is beneath the domination of the oneness of the essence. The saying, "Allah was and there was none besides Him" refers to the same state.

Ahadiyyat is a state of colourlessness, a state of the essence. The desire to acquire Ma'rifat (Gnosis) of this state does not bear any fruit. The Quran says:

> "But they shall not understand Him with their knowledge."
>
> *(Quran 20: 10)*

It is forewarned, "Allah biddeth you, beware of Him."
(Quran 3: 30)

Prophet Mohammed (PBUH) himself had said about this state "I have not known you to the extent that your knowledge demands." The Prophet had warned the thinkers, "Do not indulge in speculating on the nature of Allah, otherwise you may be destroyed." Poet, Attar, puts it in a style of his own.

> "Why exert to probe the essence of God? why strain yourself by stretching your limitations?
> When you cannot catch even the essence of an atom, how can you claim to know the essence of Allah Himself?"

Sufis call Ahadiyyat by different names. Some such names are: Ghayb-al-Ghayb (the unseen of the unseen): Munqata'al-Wijdan (the incommunicable); Ghayb-i-Huwiyyat; Ayn-i-Mutlaq (the absolute essence); Maknum-al-Muknun (the hidden of all hidden beings); Manqata-al-Isharat (one of whom of all indications are dropped); Wujud-i-bahat (pure existence); Zat-i-sadhij (colorless reality); Ayn-al-kafur (fountain of camphor), i.e. whatever gets into camphor it becomes camphor only.

Moulana Rumi, lays stress on it saying that:

What is called speculation in respect of the divine essence.

These in reality no speculation of the kind whatsoever.

The self-delusion is: for on the road to God, hundreds of thousands of obstacles interpose.

2. Wahadat (Unity)

When the mystic contemplates the being of Allah as

one who is conscious of oneself and cognizant of all the potentialities of His essence that He alone exists and as He has the potentiality of manifesting Himself, this plane is called Wahadat. It is also spoken as an "Absolute I."

In the above lines, divinity is imbedded in the words listed below:

(i) Wujud (existence)
(ii) Ilm (knowledge)
(iii) Noor (light)
(iv) Shuhud (observance)

Allah exists. He is conscious of His being, actions and attributes. He is self-revealing and self-manifest. These hypostases are spoken of a Zathi (pertaining to the essence) because they cannot be regarded as attributes. In short, they are essence itself and not super imposition on the essence. The following reasons vouchsafe the truth:

- Existence can be regarded as an attribute of essence; it would necessarily imply that the essence has precedence over existence. The precedence of the essence over existence would mean that the essence exists without existence, which is self-evidently impossible. Therefore, it is evident that existence is nothing but the essence itself and not the attribute of the essence.
- Knowledge too is identical with the essence. As the perfection of knowledge consists in encompassing its known. Knowledge will have to be admitted identical with essence.
- Light (Noor) also is identical with the essence and not the attribute of the essence.
- Observance (Shuhud) would self-evidently be regarded as identical with the essence.
- Thus, in the stage of Wuhadat, the essence would itself be in existence and the one which is conscious of its existence would be the knower, the known, and the knowledge; it would be the lighter, the lighted and the light and itself the

observer, the observed and the observance.

- Sufis of renowned eminence have given different names to this plane. It is called Tajalli-e-Awwal (first illumination) because it has manifested itself from the stage of inwardness. It is called Qabiliat-i-Awwal (first aptitude), as it is the matter of all the creatures and phenomena and all the aptitudes reveal themselves through it alone. This is also spoken as Wujud-i-Awwal (first existence) Nishan-i-Awwal (First symbol). Jawhar-i-awwal (First substance) and Khayat-i-Awwal (First thought).

3. Wahidiyyat

When the Aarif (Gnostic) contemplates the essence of Allah in all its details, covering its names (Asmaul Husna), attributes (Sifaat) and ideas together with all their aspects and their inter relationship, this plane is called Wahidiyyat (Reality of Humanity—the holy breath).

The main difference between Ahadiyyat (First epiphamy) and Wahidiyyat (second epiphany) is that of totality and its details. Details are a sort of perfection of knowledge. The plane of Ahadiyyat is called absolute, the plane of Wahadat is implicit and the plane of Wahidiyyat is explicit. Wahadat is an intermediate plane between Ahadiyyat and Wahidiyyat and in this way it combines in itself these two planes.

It is necessary to make it clear that all these three planes are called "Divine ranks." These are suppositional ranks established both from the view point of the mystic (Gnostic) as well as the Quran and Hadith. Temporal distinction is never found in them because it is evident that the absolute being would never be conceived at any moment. Allah is never unaware of His own essence, attributes, names, and ideas. Therefore, the absoluteness of essence and attributes which were found before the manifestation of things is there even after the manifestation of things. He is now as He was (Alan, Kan).

The justification made for the distinction between these

ranks is put to discussion in this way:

1. From the rational view point

Reason demands that the essence should exist first and the attributes later. This priority is of rank, not of time. Reason cannot form a conception of attributes without the conception of essence. Therefore,

> The conception of essence, regardless of its attributes, is called Ahadiyyat. This has been referred to in the Quran as, "Say: He is Allah, the one and the only."
>
> *(Quran 112: 1)*

In respect of attributes, the mystics view them first in their totality and in details, one by one.

The absolute being with the relation of detailed attributes is Wahidiyyat, i.e. with actual plurality. The Quran speaks,

> "Your Allah is one God; there is no God save Him, the beneficent the merciful."
>
> *(Quran 2: 163)*

2. From the view point of knowledge and immediate vision

The mystic gifted with perfect knowledge, knows that knowledge is included in essence and the known are included in knowledge. From the view point of entry of one object into another, the knowledge, the knower and the known are known to be identical. This is the source of distinction of the planes of Ahadiyyat, Wahadat and Wahidiyyat.

From the above discussion it should not be misunderstood that the essence had found its way in the plane of first Epiphany and came into existence or manifested itself later. All the ranks of God are eternal and are necessary for His essence; they are never separated from His essence.

In the plane of Wahidiyyat, actual plurality is taken into consideration and this plurality includes, names, attributes and divine ideas.

The zath of Allah cannot manifest itself without attributes. The essence could be discovered by attributes alone. They signify the manifestation of essence. When the essence is qualified by an attribute, it is called ISM (Name). Knowledge is the attribute of essence, Alim (knower). In short, these are not many existences but only one sole existence and its various names and attributes are really its modes.

The multiplicity of names and attributes does not cause multiplicity in the essence. Plurality would have been caused only when they had been admitted to the external existence and the independent nature of the essence. Names and attributes are only the modes. All of them have been abstracted from one essence only. And they subsist in one essence only. In the stage of essence, they are called potentialities. In the stage of knowledge, they are termed as the knowing (Ayan). In the world of phenomena, they are described as Khalq (created things).

Sufis have pointed out seven differences between the essence and the attributes. And they are:

- Logically, the essence ranks first and the attributes come next.
- The essence is self-existing and attributes depend on the essence (like wax and its softness).
- The essence is unity and the attributes display diversity.
- The essence has self-consciousness and the attributes have none.
- The essence is always hidden but the attributes are some times hidden and some times manifest.
- The manifestation of one attribute conflicts with the manifestation of another.
- The attributes must be located in their proper place.

It has been shown that in the plane of Wahadat four aspects, i.e. existence, light, knowledge and observance have no existential plurality. In the stage of Wahidiyyat, essence becomes existence (life). Knowledge of self-becomes knowledge of attributes. Light becomes will and Shuhud becomes power. Life, knowledge, will and power are the primary attributes.

From these alone have come into existence the other attributes such as hearing, sight and speech.

While discussing the creation in the preceding pages the mentioning of the word "divine ideas" or the essence of things (Al-ayan-al-Thabita) is seen. In the following pages is given a brief description of this concept.

Allah is the Knower and He has the attribute of knowledge. The attribute of knowledge in the essence of God is eternal, was eternal and will be eternal. Knowledge is possible without ideas. The knower will have the knowledge of some known objects only. The divine ideas are the essence of contingent being. All things excepting God are created. God is their Creator. He creates the Beings after knowing them. Allah's knowledge, cannot be measured or described in mere words. The created things which are known by God from eternity are but the replicas of the ideas of God. These are the essence of things which are called Al-ayan-al-Tabita. They are the determinants of divine knowledge. They possess subsistence in knowledge, and in accordance with them only, creation takes place in the external. They themselves subsist in the knowledge of Allah alone. Never do they have any external existence and they are indestructible.

Every essence has an individual aptitude of its own which is spoken of as ability. This is the essential nature by which it can be distinguished from other essences. In the terminology of the Quran, this aptitude of essence has been spoken of as "Shakilah." The Quran proclaims,

> "say: everyone acts according to his own Shakilah (disposition)."
>
> *(Quran: 17: 84)*

The essence of things is the mirror (valid proof) of the existence of God. The external world is the reflection, which is revealing itself through this mirror of the essence of things. This reflection is also called the Zil (shadow). And the shadow is revealed by light and when there is no light, it would be non-existent. So also

> the world is born out of the existence of God. The Quranic verse, "Have you not turned your vision to your Lord?" How he does prolong the shadow?" helps us in understanding this phenomenon.
>
> *(Quran 25: 45)*

The Lord has spread the relative existence, which is the shadow of the real existence on the essences of contingent things. The contingent things are in reality reflected entities, which express outwardly the essences which subsist in the knowledge of God.

The essences of things have been regarded as the mirror of God's existence. It must be noted that one of the characteristics of a mirror is that the reflection of the mirror depends on its shape and design. Another characteristic is that the mirror is not attributed with the image it reflects.

The essence of things which are the ideas of Allah resemble a mirror in which:

The being of Allah in its own immutable state manifests itself according to the aptitudes of the things. The person who is standing before a mirror remains unaltered due to the length and concavity of the mirror, so also Allah remains immutable and maintains His state. Allah will not be affected by the plurality and multiplicity of the objects through the attribute of light.

Essences are not visible in the outward world. They subsist in the divine knowledge alone. The existence of Allah has revealed itself through the forms of these essences. Whatever defect appearing in existence pertains to the inner being of the mirror.

Most of the eminent Sufis quote a Hadith which has been quite often quoted by Imam Gazali who admits its authenticity by many Muslims. It is as follows:

> "I was a hidden treasure and desired to become more and I created the world in order to be known."

The essence of Allah is a hidden treasure. It adorns the mirrors of the essences and reveal itself in those mirrors. The form of things that subsisted in Wahidiyyat was revealed in the outward plane and in them it saw itself and its own works. The above discussion can be given a technical touch as is written below:

The pure essence is the absolute state of abstract unity (Ahadiyyat) which has been referred to in the Hadith as a "secret treasure." The absolute essence, according to the absolute knowledge of the essence, is Wahadat. And according to the distributive knowledge, Wahidiyyat which consists of brief observance and comprises detail observations. Therefore, essence is independent of all other existences. The Quran says:

> "Allah is altogether independent of His creatures. The essence beholds His own being and is independent of the manifestation of attributes and can do without the world."

The Sufis call it Kamal-i-Zati (Perfection of essence). Ahadiyyat, Wahadaat and Wahidiyyat are the divine ranks. These are the internal ranks of the essence.

For revealing the Kamal-i-Asmai (perfection of the names), Allah desired to observe His totality and detail in the external, just as they observe in the internal stages, He made the world. By making the world means, He manifested Himself in the form of the essences of things. The details of external mundane planes are presented which are detailed description of the worlds of "Soul", "Similitude" and "Body."

These are the comprehensive stages of man. The above description may mislead one into believing the individualization of the absolute being. By actualization of the potential, the world is not excluded from the essence of God. Neither is a void created in it. The essence remains the same as it was before. A summary of this technical expression is given in the following poetry:

> "He has rendered the world into a mirror wherein He shows Himself unto Himself. All that is in and unseen is but a reflection of His beauty!
> When that beauty desired to come in the form of Glory,

It put on the visage of this world as time and space!
Whose is any name?
Whose is any identity?
Is there anything, here and there other than Him?
He alone is there under every name and under every identity."

Haqq is manifest in the form of actual things and things exist through the real existence of Haqq. This manifestation is of three kinds:

- The manifestation of the abstract as the manifestation of the essence of Allah in the multiple Asma-e-Hasna.
- The manifestation of the abstract as the manifestation of the soul in the multiple parts of the body.
- The manifestation of the matter as the manifestation of a single person in multi-coloured mirrors.

In all the above three illustrations it cannot be conceived that the division or unity is possible in the very nature of that which manifests itself.

The relation found between the manifest and the manifested; between the Rubb and Abd and the Creator and the created beings is quite different from all other relations.

This relationship is neither pure "otherness" nor pure identity. This relationship is explained thus:

Pure otherness: If we regard the relationship between Haqq and Khalq as real, we will have to assume the relationship between the carpenter and furniture. This interpretation is not supported by Quaranic verses and the Hadith quoted above.

Pure identity: This relationship is the opposite of the above. Here, the relationship of identity between Haqq and Khalq is regarded as literal. According to it, the relationship between Haqq and Khalq is the same, as found between wax and its different shapes, or between a sea and its waves.

The Holy Quran posits the essence of the Abd as the

other and regards the essence of the Abd as a supplicant, a trustee, and a vicegerent. The essence of Abd is purely a mendicant, existence does not originally belong to him. He is a trustee. When he employs the divine trust in the universe he is called vicegerent of God. These only are the pure aspects of the Abd, i.e. trust, and vicegerency Now he should make an effort to face himself in the essence of Allah on which depends his perfection. This is his internal striving called Raza-E-Ilahi. When he moves in this path, the Abd passes away. Allah alone remains. When a man reaches this stage, there is neither Creator nor the creatures; neither the knower nor the known and neither the lover nor the loved. All this he has to do not by shunning the world, but by facing the reality of the world and remaining within the world.

In no stage Abdiyat be dispensed with. So long as one lives and retains reasoning, it is compulsory to follow shariah. Abdiyat alone is the cause of freedom. The question that arises is: What is freedom? It is to cut oneself off absolutely from everything other than Allah. True freedom is enjoyed by the man who establishes a relationship of Abdiyat with Allah.

In the foregoing pages it is pointed out that the essences of things are the mirrors of existence of Allah and the external world is the reflection which is revealing itself through the mirrors. These essences are the ideas of Allah. They exist in the knowledge of Allah and hence essences are the divine aspects. So is the case with the essence of human beings, i.e. Rooh (spirit) or divine breath of Allah. Describing the creation of human being the Quran says:

> "Then when I have formed him and breathed into him My spirit,.......
>
> *(Quran 15:29)*
>
> "So when I have fashioned him and breathed into him My (created) soul ...
>
> *(Quran 38:72)*

According to the Quran, Allah created Adam from dust and breathed into him His own spirit. This is the essence of human beings which subsists in the mind of Allah and exists in the knowledge of Allah. Therefore, a human being is born with potentialities to recognize his creator and to receive divine revelation, to act according to His commandments and to enact deeds to please his Creator. According to Islam, human nature is potentially good and it is on its account that it rises high towards its ideal of serving his Creator pleasing his Creator, by all his worldly acts. Prophet Mohammed (PBUH) is reported to have said:

> "Every child belongs to one faith or the other", his parents turn him to one faith or the other."
>
> *(Bukhari and. Muslim)*

Moreover, the potential goodness of human soul is a direct corollary of the divine breath in human beings. According to Quran, the sin of Adam was pardoned by Allah, when he repented. The Quran mentions this sin only as an accident in the life of Adam and not as an eternal curse affecting the entire human beings.

But it is to be remembered that the human soul is good only potentially. Like a seed, it is merely a possibility of developing into an oak, if the soil and the climate are favourable. It has still to actualize its possibilities. Human effort is needed to get back to the original oneness of the human soul when it was created. The ways and means to avoid to so many temptations and hindrances in the way of its progress will be discussed in the next chapter along with a profile on purification of the soul. This in a nutshell is the Islamic Theory of Human Motivation.

ISLAMIC CONCEPTUALIZATION OF HUMAN MOTIVATION VS. WESTERN CONCEPTUALIZATION

Western theories of motivation begin with the basic assumption that the human being who it is part of animal nature has certain needs which are to be gratified. According to their conceptualization it is the need fulfilment which serves as the springboard for motivated behaviour. The moment the needs fulfilled, the human beings get satisfied.

Among the various theories of Western Motivation reviewed in Chapter-III, the only theory of motivation which discusses the motivation based on human nature is the Need Hierarchy Theory of Motivation propounded by Abraham Maslow. According to this theory, the ultimate need is self-actualization and it stops with that.

What is the conceptualization of self-actualization in Islamic framework? This question will be answered in the following pages.

By, 'self' the Western theories mean potentiality of human being, the Quran accepts this conceptualization:

> "Say, everyone acts according to his own Shakila. (Disposition or aptitude)."
>
> *(Quran 17:84)*

Iqbal, the mystic poet, has expressed the same idea of self-actualization in the following words:

> "It is the inward reach of a thing, its realizable possibilities which lie within the depth of its nature, serially actualize themselves."
> (Reconstruction of Religious Thoughts in Islam, by Allama Iqbal)

Iqbal's concept of Khudi is something similar to self-actualization of Western behavioural thinkers. In the following couplet, Iqbal presents his view of Khudi:

> Raise thyself to such heights,
> that before every fate befalls,
> God shall ask you to say,
> what do you propose to ordain for yourself?

However, as has been pointed out in the Islamic theory of motivation, self-actualization is not the summum bonum of life. Its terminal value is Raza-e-Ilahi. It is transcending one's-self. Self-transcendence and not self-actualization is the Islamic concept of motivation.

However, it should not be construed that the

actualization of one's potentials has no relevance in Islamic scheme of things. Man should become what he is capable of becoming, but he should do it to please his Creator, his Master, his Lord. The Western conceptualization of self-actualization falls short of explaining self-actualization for what? And Islam has the real answer and the only answer is that man should do it for pleasing Allah. When a human-being reaches this stage, experientially finite ego gets so emerged in the Supreme Ego. Man's ego in its every action/ work experiences the Absolute Ego. Every act of man becomes the act of God. Man operating at his stage, hits the plateau of mystical experience. This may be described as *fauna* (merger of man's ego in the Absolute Ego, at least experientially). It may be viewed as experiential self-transdence. Through training infinite ego reaches this experience. Training methods are described in the next chapter.

5

*Cultural Intervention Strategy**

In this chapter, an attempt is made to present a sketch of methods suggested by Islamic theologists and mystics to bring about the required change in the human being as well as in an organizational member. The Islamic theory of motivation, articulated in the previous chapter, points out that the ultimate aim of human life is to seek Allah's pleasure. Though the human being has innate urge to recognize his Creator, to seek His pleasure and to get salvation, it must be pointed out that this urge will not actualize on its own, without going through the process of actualization. This chapter discusses the process of making a human being what he is expected to be in the light of Islamic teachings.

Taskiya-e-Nafs (Purification of Self)

The very purpose of sending prophets to guide mankind is to do Taskiya-e-Nafs (Purification of self). Prophet

* The researcher have drawn extensively from the works of various authorities of Islam in Urdu, Arabic and English languages. All such books and journals are listed out in the Bibliography. However, no citation is given in this chapter as the authors have expressed their own views on the cultural intervention strategy in this chapter. To all those authors whose copious literature has been utilized, the authors express their gratitude.

Ebrahim (PBUH) praying to his Lord for the need of sending Prophet Mohammed (PBUH) requested in the following words:

> "Our Lord send among them an apostle of their own, who shall rehearse your signs to them and instrument them in scripture and wisdom and purify them: for you are the exalted in might, the wise."
>
> *(Quran 2: 1-9)*

As per the wishes of Prophet Ebrahim, Prophet Mohammed (PBUH) was sent for the guidance of mankind. Describing the mission of Prophet Mohammed, the Holy Quran says:

> "a similar (favour) have you already received. In that we have sent among you an apostle of your own, rehearse him to use our signs, and purifying you and instructing you in scripture and wisdom and in new knowledge."
>
> *(Quran 2: 151)*

Stressing the mission of Prophet Mohammed (PBUH), Allah (SWT) has said, in Holy Quran;

> "It is he who has sent among the illiterates an apostle from among themselves, who rehearse to them his signs, to purify them and to instruct them in scripture and wisdom although they had been, before, in manifest error."
>
> *(Quran 57: 2)*

From the above verses of the Holy Quran, it is clear that the ultimate purpose of the prophethood is the purification of soul. Though instruction in wisdom, and the recitation of the scripture are mentioned, they do not constitute the ultimate objective of the prophethood. Giving instructions in scripture, and training human beings in wisdom are all instrumental in the ultimate goal of purification of soul.

In sending other Prophets of Islam who guide the mankind, Allah emphasizes the purification of human soul as the summum bonum of the Prophet's mission. Allah points out the goal of Moosa (Alaihi Wassalam), saying,

> "You go to Pharoah, for he has indeed transgressed all bounds; and say to him 'why don't you get purified (from sin)?"
>
> *(Quran 79: 17-18)*

The very purpose of all the Prophets was sanctification of the souls. The human being's salvation, Falah in life here after hinges upon purification of nafs. All the efforts of the Prophets were directed towards purification of the human soul. The Holy Quran testifies to the fact that the human being cannot attain salvation unless his soul is purified. In another place the Holy Quran puts this beautifully in the following verse;

> "Truly he succeeds that purifies it, and he fails that corrupts it."
>
> *(Quran 91: 9-10)*

Evidently, when Allah pointed out that one's success depended upon his purification of soul, it is but natural that the Prophets who were sent for bringing salvation to humanity should have any other purpose, than Taskiye-Nafs (Purification of self). Not only Prophet Mohammed [PBUH] but all the Prophets were sent specifically for the purification of the human soul.

MEANING OF PURIFICATION

In Arabic language, Taskiya means cleaning, it also means, development, it connotes growth and also refers to the nurturing and strengthening of all qualities within the human self that are essential for growth and development.

Purification of self means, removal of all evil passions, getting rid of bad ideologies and the purging of all the evil qualities which have taken root in self. All the irrational fears and unwarranted desires need to be driven out. It is a type of treatment of the self in which the human mind is open to rational thinking, Spiritual and moralistic growth occurs only when the human self is purified. The morality of the human being will reach its perfection, only through purification of soul. In short, man should get back to that status where he has no desire or no motive other than pleasing Allah. It is to make man possess a soul of purity which he was proud enough to have in his infancy.

The Holy Quran itself defines Taskiya-e-Nafs,

> "By the soul, and the proportion and the order given to it, and gets enlightenment as to its wrong and right, truly who succeeds that purifies it."
>
> *(Quran: 91: 7-9)*

It is made clear that Allah has corrected man from taking the wrong path of evils forces by commanding him to work along the royal highway of pity, piety and purity. This is the most precious gift of all to man—the faculty of distinguishing between the right and wrong. He who makes an effort to look at the things in their proper perspective will be a successful person.

TAZKIYA (Purification)—ALL EMBRACING PROCESS

Islam does not subscribe to the type of asceticism in which we purify our hearts and yet remain immersed in political, economic or social corruption. Tazkiya must encompass our entire life—the privacy of thoughts as well as their social manifestations in our daily life. Everything must be in conformity with Allah's will.

Unless we tap Tazkiya process, we will find that our lives are compartmentalized, certain parts impending the development of others. This can only result in a life of disharmony and unhappiness. Tazkiya should be approached as a comprehensive and all-embracing process.

The process of Tazkiya will not only purify our hearts but also influence our entire life and the will of Allah will become so much easier for us to follow. Following the divine will in its verbatim is Tazkiya itself. All our efforts will be directed towards the ultimate goal—the pleasure of Allah.

> "It is God, who causes whomever he wills to grow in purify; and none shall be wronged by as much as a hair's breadth."
>
> *(Quran 4: 49)*

> "Where it not for God's favour upon you and his grace, not one of you would ever have remained pure. For it is God who causes whomever He wills to grow in purity; for God is All-Hearing, All-Knowing."
>
> *(Quran 24: 21)*

Thus, Tazkiya does not consist simply of ideas, but of life, behaviour and conduct.

WHAT IS NAFs?

Nafs [Self] is a force which is attached to the Rooh [Soul] and it is a composite part of man. The Nafs would concern itself mainly with the needs of the body. But it also tries to keep the body in comfort and ease. It attempts to fulfil human needs, desires and materialistic requirements. The Nafs *per se* is not all evil. The Nafs inclines towards evilness when it loses its moralistic criteria, i.e. right and wrong.

The Holy Quran points out the evil in Nafs:

> "Verily the Nafs ever urges to evil, except that Nafs on whom my lord has mercy; verily my lord is forgiving and merciful."
>
> —*Quran*

The Nafs is short-sighted and concerned with immediate needs. It does not have higher concepts, noble thoughts that the Rooh is blessed with.

The relationship between the Rooh and Nafs and the body is illustrated in the following parable. A traveller sets out on an important journey from an unknown place to an important destination. He is given a horse as his only means of conveyance. If the horse is wild and not controlled, it will become unmanageable. If the traveller attempts to ride on it, it will try to throw him off and break lose. The horse would like nothing better than freedom, so that it can go freely with its herd of wild horses, concern only with eating and frolicking with the mares unrestrictedly and can try to become the leader of the herd.

If the rider allows the horse to run wild, the least that will happen is that the horse will take him away from the straight path. The worst things that will happen is that he will be thrown-off in some remote area. He will not be able to reach his destination.

The other side of the coin is to give some amount of training to the horse, so that it becomes tame and obedient, and will take the traveller to his destination.

In imparting training the rider must be careful not to go to extremes. Free reign given to the horse would be as bad as depriving it of food and water.

The situation of the rider is like that of the Rooh. The Rooh has to make its journey to Allah. The horse is like one's body, the vehicle given to the Rooh, where as mind controlling the actions of the horse is similar to one's Nafs. Nafs and the human body are required to complete Rooh's journey successfully.

CLASSIFICATION OF NAFs

There are 3 States of Nafs:

1. Nafsul Ammara,
2. Nafsul Lowwama, and
3. Nafsul Muthmainna.

(I) Nafsul Ammara

"I do not acquit myself, (that myself is above evil), verily the (human) self ever urges to evil, except that self on whom my lord has mercy; verily my Lord is Forgiving, Merciful."

(Quran 12: 53)

This Nafs is indisciplined, and beyond control, leading to evils and sins. One can easily know whether the Nafs is Ammara or not. The beautiful answer given is if one does not repent over one's evil deeds, it should be recognized as Nafsul Ammara. In this stage of Nafs, all the motives described by various organizational theorists, and psycho analysts hold good. As pointed out by Sigmond Fraued, the mind reaches out to libido. Employees in whom Nafsul Ammara is operating at lower levels of needs or baser needs such as need for power, need for autonomy, need for destruction will be ruining their soul.

While describing about human needs, the holy Quran says:

> "Attractive in the eyes of men is the love of things they aspire: women and sons; heaped up hoards of gold and silver; horses, branded [for excellence] and wealth of cattle and fertile land. Such are possession of this world's life but in nearness to God is the best of the goals [to return to]."
>
> *(Quran 3: 14)*

When a person operates at the level of Nafsul Ammara, he does not transcend beyond baser needs such as sex, wealth, snobbish articles, etc. Allah points out that for Nafsul Ammara all these needs are made attractive. The motivational basis of a man with Nafsul Ammara is to seek gratification of sex, hoards of riches, etc. In a business organizational context, members of an organization with Nafsul Ammara will be motivated by money, bread, prestige status, etc. They cease to go beyond these lower order motives.

(2) Nafsul Lowwama

> "And I swear by accusing soul, (which blames him when he falls into sin or error."
>
> *(Quran 75: 2)*

When the Nafs progresses to Lowwama, the battle

between the Rooh and Nafs starts. The Rooh tries to control the Nafs. If the Rooh is able to control the Nafs, it is termed as Jihad-e-Akbar. The battle between Rooh and Nafs is perennial. Some times, the Rooh overpowers the Nafs and at times, the Nafs takes a lead.

The following are the signs to confirm that the Nafs is operating at Lowwama level.

Weak needs can easily be given up, but strong desires are always irresistible; keeping certain motives under control but falling a victim to certain other motives is like sailing in troubled waters.

A man operating at Lowwama will be a better person. He satisfies sexual urge to the extent permitted by Islamic sharia; he tries to acquire enough wealth to take care of his worldly needs, and his family members.

(3) Nafs-ul-Muthmainna

This is the stage in which the Nafs, rebellious in nature, overtakes the individual. Nafs is totally disciplined. The Rooh and the Nafs are inclined towards love of Allah and always seek His pleasure.

This is the highest evolution of the Nafs and in this state there is not much striking difference between the Rooh and the Nafs.

When the stage is Muthmainna it receives a call from Allah to come to His abode of peace,

> "[To the righteous soul will be said:]
> "O (Thou) soul, In (complete) rest and satisfaction!
> come back thou, to thy lord—
> well pleased (thyself) and well pleasing unto Him!
> "Yea, enter then my Heaven!
>
> *(Quran 89: 27-30)*

The inner experience of the soul of Muthmainna always delights in communication with the Creator. Such human beings far exceed opens in the execution of work. If he happens to be a manager he will be on alert at planning, organizing, staffing, etc. and will harvest better results on the lines of those with Nafsul Ammara and Nafsul Lowwama.

Nafsul Muthmainna does not mean an ascetic behaviour, for asceticism is not in conformity with Islamic culture.

It is the soul's joyful experience that triggers the individual to excel in his work. This gets manifested in the outer world in the form of increasing market -share, improving bottom line, working for the best EPS (Earning per share) and accelerating the organization's performance and his own performance. All he/she does, is not to satisfy or fulfil his/her motives but to satisfy his/her inner urge to present the best picture of himself or herself when he/she has the chance of meeting Him in the Akhirath. This is something totally different from the concept of motivation of western literature which proclaims that actions spring from fulfilment of certain needs and wants and here action stems from the basic need of seeking His pleasure.

The researcher is presenting an outline of the training programme formulated by Islam, for graduating the Nafsul Ammara to Nafsul-Muthmainna. There are two primary streams of training programmes available in Islamic thought. One school of thought led by the Theologists which emphasizes on the belief system, knowledge and virtuous life (Amale-Saliha). It does not address itself to individual psychology and its main thrust is on social psychology. On the other hand the Islamic mystics (Sufia) have prescribed a training programme, technics, and methods. The readers may decide which method to follow depending upon his individual needs. To be sure, both the approaches are part and parcel of Islamic framework, based on the Quran and Sunnah. They differ in the matter of inferences and details.

I. ISLAMIC THEOLOGICAL APPROACH

The Muslim theologists who belong to the main stream have prescribed ways and means of transforming the Nafs into Muthmainnal Nafs. A brief description of this approach is attempted in the pages to follow.

Objective of the Science of Tazkiya

This science focuses attention on all aspects of human life. It points out all the evil desires of human beings and suggests a solution to getting rid of these passions. It positively suggests the behaviour of the Nafs to seek the pleasure of God, which is the ultimate goal of a human being.

The seeker of Nafsul Muthamainna should neither be over joyful during prosperity, and should not feel disappointed in adversity. Whatever be the position of life, whatever be the situation, he should always be contended with Allah. The seeker of Muthmainna should be like a rock of purpose even when he is rocked by sorrows failures and despairs. Even in the moments of overwhelming joy, he should not budge even an inch from his primary aim.

Methods of purification

Theologists are of the opinion that the following two methods are sufficient for purification of self.

1. Purification of Knowledge

A human being should acquire sufficient knowledge about his existential issues. He should seek answers to all those questions which are necessary for making his ideological moorings, inclinations, standards, values so that he can get back to the straight path (sirathe musthaqeem) if he has deviated from it and stick on to the straight path if he is already on it. For example, he should ask him self who he is and where from he has come. He should ask himself whether he is the Creator of the created. He should be aware of his close ties with the Creator. He should be knowing the attributes of his Creator. If he knows these things, he will surely be safeguarding his Nafs (self) from his deviations towards the wrong path.

2. Purification of Deeds

Man has to work constantly to earn his bread. He should go on working all through his life. But his activities, either good or bad, will have their impact on him.

The theologists refer to these activities as the permitted (Halal) and the prohibited (Haram). Their main thrust is on the motivational aspect of these activities. An activity may be motivated by several motives. They suggest the motives are to be encouraged and those that are to be discarded.

Deeds, however significant they are, will have no credit unless they spring from pious-motives. For example, charity. An individual may give charity so as to gain popularity, and to maintain his social status. It may be his fancy or it may be an altruistic motive of sincerity. Islamic theology harbours not only the behavioural aspect of human beings but also the motives that shape or influence their behaviour.

Motives which are repugnant to Islamic spirit need to be replaced by motives that are altruistic, i.e. the desire to please one's Lord. This in the eyes Islamic theology, is purification of the self.

Source of the real knowledge

According to Islamic Theology, the signboard of true knowledge is recognizing one's God. When Islamic theology advocates deliberations on knowledge, it is not the knowledge of faculties such as chemistry, botany, physiology or social sciences such as economics, finance, history, management, etc. The main emphasis is on acquiring divine knowledge. The Theologists wonder what benefit they get from learning science without mastering the science of self. As Rumi says pertinently; one have turned into a philosopher but

"YOU KNOW NOT"
Where you are? From where you have come?
And what your are?
O, poor man! When you know not yourself,
Why, then do you pride your self on
The so-called knowledge?"

Therefore, the main thrust of Muslim Theology is that one should acquire knowledge about his existential issues. It describes existential issues such as recognizing Allah, life after death, revelation, prophet-hood, etc.

Recognising Allah (Ma'rifat)

Man is able to enjoy the paradise peace and joy only when he knows Allah [Marifat]. One must acquire sound and sensible knowledge about the existence of Allah, His attributes, His likes and dislikes, His dealings with individuals, groups and societies, etc.

The Islamic Theology brings home the fact that there are different stages of Marifat. It is surprising that get closer to Allah and some others may recognize Him as Allah, but theology stresses emphatically that, it is not within the reach of human beings to see Allah or to get any idea about His essence [Zath].

The Holy Quran says, "And remember when you said: "O Moosa! we shall never believe in you till we see Allah plainly. So, then and there a thunderbolt (lightning) seized you and this scene also you have witnessed. And you were laid lifeless: even after that we raised you (after that death), so that you may offer your gratitude's."

(Quran 2: 55-56)

From these verses it is obvious that with the existing body no man can see Allah. Man may get knowledge about Allah from His sings and attributes.

Similarly, Prophet Moosa (PBUH) wanted to see Allah and know His essence. Allah replied that he could not withstand the vision of Him. Allah warned that even mountains cannot with stand His Tajalli (manifestation).

The Holy Quran refers to this incident in the following verse:

> "And when Moosa came at our appointment, and his Lord spoke to him; Moosa said: "O my Lord!" Show me that I may look at you! Allah said: "you cannot see me; but remain looking upon the mountain, if it stands still in its place on my manifestation, then you shall be capable to see me." So when Moosa's Lord manifested His splendour in the mountain, it collapsed to dust; and Moosa fell down unconscious. Then when he recovered his senses, he said: "Glory be to you! I turn repentant, and I am the first of the believers."
>
> *(Quran 7: 143)*

Muslim theologists have classified recognition (ma'rifat) into three types:

- The first stage of recognition is to know His attributes described by Himself as well as by the Prophets.

- The second stage of recognition is to know that there is no difference between His essence and His attributes.
- The third stage of recognition is to recognize His hand, His decisions, in short, HIM in every aspect of human life. Neither logic nor philosophy nor the mediator can help in this process. It is totally a personal experience.

The best way of getting marifat of Allah is through His books and the Prophets. WAHI-E-ILAHI (Revelation) alone should be accepted as the only source of knowledge (AL-ILM).

Islamic theology recognizes only two sources of knowledge: (a) The Holy Quran, and (b) The life of Prophet Mohammed [SAW]. [Wuswa-e-Hasna]

The Holy Quran

It was pointed out earlier that marifat-e-Ilahi can be obtained from AL-ILM, the knowledge. The primary source of knowledge is the Holy Quran.

The Book of the Creator of Universe has underlined the objective of human life and emphasized the importance of purity of motives. The researcher has drawn the following verses from the Holy Quran to bring out the altruistic motivational basis in Islam.

> The Holy Quran says: "And I have not created jinn and man except that they should serve me."
>
> *(Quran 51: 56)*

> "And whosoever desires in the hereafter and strives for it, with the necessary efforts due for it, while he is a believer as well, then such are the ones whose striving shall be appreciated (by Allah)."
>
> *(Quran 17: 19)*

Thus, every man should struggle hard to please his master. Intention to seek the pleasure of Allah, in all our actions, is like alchemy, which turns everything into gold.

Every action anchoring on the intention bears fruits and so is every utterance no good will go unnoticed and unrewarded. Such an idea in mind creates a wonderful mental force which nobody in the world can check. Such a man is born to serve Allah, lives for Allah, thinks for Allah, acts for Allah and speaks for Allah. Such a man is, therefore, said to be in the way of Allah. The Holy Quran says:

> "Whether wage I might have asked of you is yours; my wage is with Allah; (repudiating any suggestion of worldly gain or interest on his part); and He is witness of everything)."
> Such a person does not seek any worldly reward "except seeking the pleasure of his Lord, the most high."
>
> *(Quran 92: 20)*

> To reach the object of love of Allah is the goal of a human being. The Quran teaches the holy Prophet as well as the Muslims to declare "My prayer, my sacrifice, my life, and my death are all for Allah, the Lord of the world."
>
> *(Quran 6: 136)*

He who has such a vision will be crowned with success.

Man's love for fame, power, wealth are so great that he cannot resist the temptation of such attractions towards these things. The Holy Quran speaks of such persons who worship fame, people and other things besides Allah:

> "And these are some among men who take for themselves objects of worship, besides Allah, whom they love as they love Allah."
>
> *(Quran: 2: 165)*

One should approach the holy book without any bias. His motive should be to get guidance (Hidayath) and marifath (recognition) of Allah. If a person approaches the Holy Quran without the intention of recognizing Allah, the

Quran will not reveal or illuminate his heart with marifat-e-Ilahi.

The Quran is to be accepted as the source book of knowledge. It should be approached as a Holy book and it has originated from the Creator and the primary source of knowledge.

One could get the real benefit from the holy verses only when he approaches the Quran with the burning desire to change his life according to the teachings of the book. He should be prepared to change his values, standards, character, ideological thinking strictly in the height of its teachings.

Life of Prophet Muhammed [PBUH]

WUSWA-E-HASNA

Another authentic source of recognizing Allah (marif-e-Ilahi) and purification of self (Tazkiya-e-Nafs) is the life of Prophet Mohammed (PBUH). Muslim theologists have stressed the role - model of Prophet Mohammed's (SAW) character alone for the complete guidance of mankind. He was the symbol of modesty, sincerity, truthfulness and true devotion to Allah in seeking His pleasure and there by setting the highest example of human excellence.

> "Certainly there is for you in the messenger of Allah an excellent example."
>
> *(Quran 33: 21)*

The life and achievements of Prophet Mohammed (PBUH) are but the Holy Quran in practice. The Holy Quran contains abstract principles of Islam. We have to get the details of these principles from the sayings and deeds of the Holy Prophet. It is, therefore, necessary for us to study the sayings of the Holy Prophet who had mercy for both the worlds. The Holy Quran describes in the following words:

> "And we have not sent you except as a mercy and to the worlds."
>
> *(Quran 21: 107)*

Purification of Deeds

By purification of deeds, theologists mean that the intention behind the actions should be pure. It is the motive which determines the purity of deeds. Sometimes, an action may be highly pious, but a deeper enquiry may reveal that the intention behind deeds may be evil. For example, in an organization an employee may be over working for the progress of the organization. An in-depth analysis may reveal that he may be doing with the intention of spoiling the good image of one of his colleagues.

Precisely, this is the reason why Islam attaches importance not just to deeds but also to the intention. A person's pious deeds may not worth any reward in the eyes of Allah if it has not been done with a good intention. In Islam, only that work is accepted which emanates from the sincerity of motives.

The following Hadith of Prophet Mohammed (SAW) brings out the importance of motivational purity in Islamic culture:

The message of Allah as reported by Omar-bin-al-Khattab reads that, actions are to be judged by intention. There is surely in man what he intends. So, whosoever's emigration is to Allah and his apostle, whosoever's emigration is to the world which he seeks or to a woman whom he marries, his emigration is to that for which he makes emigration.

Mishkat-ul-Masabih

The importance of purity of motive in Islam can be understood from the fact that sometimes in the account of a person an evil deed is added just because he has had the intention of doing it. Similarly, in the account of a person a noble deed gets recorded just because he has such a good intention.

The following traditions of Prophet Mohammed (PBUH) illustrate the importance of motives in Islamic framework:

> The words of Hadrath Ayesha (RAL) as reported by Muwajiah, "I have certainly heard the messenger of

Allah say: Who seeks pleasure of Allah with displeasure of men, Allah will be sufficient for him as a protector from men."

—*Tirmizi*

Abu Hurairah reported that the messenger of Allah had said: Surely, the first man who will be brought for judgment on the resurrection day will be one who had been (well-known as) a martyr. He will be brought and be reminded of the favours on him, which he will recognize. He will say that he had fought for Allah and laid down his life as a martyr. Allah will chide him for telling lies. He tells that the so called martyr had fought as he was named as a hero. He put-up a brave fight to prove himself to be great hero and not to serve God. The judgment will be against him and he will be dragged downwards thrown into hell.

Another will be the man who acquired knowledge and taught it (to men) and read the Quran. He will be brought for judgment and be reminded of the favours on him, which he will recognize. Allah will ask him: what he did and he will reply saying that he had acquired learning and taught it and read the Quran for Allah. And Allah will tell him that he had spoken falsehood, and he had acquired learning that he might be called a learned man and he had read the Quran that he might be called a reader, like the first one he too will be dragged down to be thrown into Hell.

Another man whom Allah gave ample wealth and whom he gave of every description will be brought and be reminded of the favours on him, which he will recognize. Allah will repeat the question what he did when he was alive. The wealthy one answers that he had spent huge sums of money by way of giving charity. Allah will tell that the wealthy fellow had done so only to be called a philanthropist. Then the order will be passed against him and he will be dragged down and thrown into Hell.

—*Muslim*

Jaber-bin-Atik reported that the Apostle of Allah said: As for anger, there is something which Allah loves and something which Allah hates. As for that which Allah loves, it is anger in doubtful things; and as for boast, there is something which Allah hates and something which Allah loves, it is the boast of a man at the time for fight in Allah's cause, and his boast at the time of charity; and as for that which Allah hates, it is his boast in pedigree.

—*Ahmad, Abu Daud, Nasai*

Abu Hurairrah reported that the Messenger of Allah had said: People will be raised up according to their intentions.

—*Ibn Majah*

Abu Hurairah reported that the messenger of Allah had said: Allah looks not to your figures, nor to your wealth, but He looks at your hearts and deeds.

—*Muslim*

Abu Bakr (RAL) reported that the messenger of Allah had said: When two Muslims encounter with their swords, then the killer and the killed are both in the Fire. I asked: O messenger of Allah this is about the murderer; but why is it so with regard to the one murdered? He said, "Because he was greatly desirous of killing his companion."

—*Agreed*

Abu Hurairah reported that the messenger of Allah had said: Whoever marries a woman for a dower with the intention of not paying it back, is a fornicator, and whoever takes a loan with the intention of not returning he is a thief.

—*Ibn Majah*

From the above discussion it is clear that Muslim theologists emphasize that the motive should be to seek the pleasure of Allah. They suggest that:

(i) Remembrance of Allah (Zikhre Ilahi), and
(ii) Concern for here-after (Fikr-e-Akirath)

will purify one's motive to seek the pleasure of Allah.

(i) Remembrance of Allah [Zikr-e-Ilahi]

In every mode of our life we should remember Allah. Prophet Mohammed (SAW) has taught us different prayers [Duas] to say at every point of life of the human beings, right from starting any work to going on a pilgrimage. This remembrance of Allah should be kept with full knowledge of it. Never it should be a formal affair—

> Whenever a human being forgets Allah, he forgets himself. He fails to remember the purpose of his life; the one who has created him, the supreme one who has gifted him the worldly bounties; the matchless one who has provided him the required skills. When he forgets Allah, he will run after the desires of his Nafs. For our spiritual development, it is necessary that one should remember Allah always. The remembrance of Allah gives a peace of mind that cannot be described in words. The Holy Quran says: "Indeed! In the remembrance of Allah, hearts do find comfort."
>
> *(Quran 13: 28)*

(ii) Concern for Hereafter [Fikr-e-Akirath]

The concern for hereafter is one aspect of remembrance of Allah. The natural corollary of remembrance of Allah is to remember the life hereafter. A man always keeps the ultimate goal of life that is Falah-e-Akirath (success in the hereafter] man is mortal and death is certain. The parts of glory and valour lead but to the grave. The world is illusory and so is our existence. One must remember and revere the bounties of life hereafter and fear the punishments hereafter. Right action and staunch faith (Amal-e-saleha) alone will lead to success in the life hereafter.

II. ISLAMIC MYSTIC'S APROACH

The Sufi's main aim is cleaning the Nafs. Evidently different schools of thought of Islamic mystics have endeavored to develop an elaborate training programme. They call such training programme Mujahadah. It means to act contrary to the dictates of one's wavering Nafs, at the time of seeking Allah's pleasure. It is the right way of opposing one's Nafs so that it can be tamed at the time of seeking Allah's pleasure and obeying His commands.

Not all the demands of Nafs are unlawful. Those needs which are essential for the growth and maintenance of life are lawful requirements of the Nafs. The purpose of Mujaahada is to discipline the Nafs to the extent that it is contented with the essentials. It has no desire for anything in excess, even though it is permitted in Islamic law.

What is not Mujaahadah?

Unfortunately, some people have the wrong opinion about the Mujaahadah. They believe in giving up worldly activities, going to jungles, mountains and leading an ascetic life and such non fulfilment of the requirements of the body is Mujaahadah. But the following are not considered to be Mujaahadah.

Weakening the NAFs

To weaken the Nafs to the extent that its basic rights are denied is against the teachings of Prophet Mohammed (PUBH). A Hadith says "verily, your Nafs has a right over you."

Frustrating NAFs

> A frustrated Nafs loses its utilitarian value and gets decayed. Over burdening is not the aim of Islam. Allah says time and again "we do not impose more burden than what a Nafs can bear."
>
> *(Quran: 2: 21.86)*

It is the principle of convincing balance between the needs of Nafs and the urge to seek the pleasure of God.

TYPES OF MUJAAHADAH

Nafsaani Mujaahadah: The purpose of this Mujahadah is to prevent Nafs from turning to evil. Preventing a man from committing sin is the real purpose of Mujaahadah.

Jismaani Mujaahada: Certain exercises are prescribed in order to accustom and habituate the Nafs to simple living. When austerity becomes the second nature of man, he abstains even from lawful pleasures, and there will be a lesser probability of approaching anything doubtful. Such people do never like to be in touch with the unlawful.

The purpose of Mujaahadah Jismani is to rise man to the level of Mujaahade Nafsani.

THE PRINCIPLES OF MUJAAHADAH

I. NAFSANI MUJAHADA

The two fundamental principles relating to the intellect are:

(A) Opposing the Nafs when it leans towards sin, and
(B) Compelling the Nafs to do pious deeds.

(A) To act contrary to the Nafs when it is inclined towards sin. In other words, getting rid of Akhlaaqe-Razeelah (Debasing Qualities). The following are the evil qualities, which have to be got rid of:

(i) HIRS (Greed)

Greed is a total attachment to and obsession with materialism. Greed has no end point like a fire raging more and more as additional fuel is fed into it. He who is greedy person will never be content with what he has already amassed. Greed is the root cause of all ills. It leads to arrogance, lust and other evil traits. This affects the Nafs as well as the body. Dishonesty, strife, depression, mania are some of the ill effects of Hirs.

Prevention

Prophet Mohammed (PBUH) has advised muslims to look to the needs of the deprived sections of the society to understand Allah's bounty.

- Be content with what Allah has granted.

- Avoid obsession with events in the remote future.
- Recognize and admit that Hirs is despicable.

Treatment

Not to show-off. Allah wants us not to indulge in conspicuous spending/snobbish spending. Allah identities this expenditure with the mischevious acts of Shaitan.

Allah wants man to act against one's Nafs when it desires Haram.

TAMA (Avarice)

This is a stage beyond Hirs. If Tama is not controlled, one may fall prey to the deadly sins of shirk and Kufr.

Prevention and treatment

The same measures prescribed for Hirs are applicable here.

(ii) GHUSSAH (Anger)

Anger is an emotion caused by some ill-feeling. Uncontrolled anger leads to rage, quarrels, hatred, violence and a host of other evil doings.

Prevention

Develop sabr (patience).

Treatment

Prophet Mohammed (PBUH) gives a list of simple instruction to get rid of anger:

(a) Make Wudhu (ablution) with cold water.
(b) If an angry person is standing he should get seated.
(c) If an angry person is sitting he should lie down for a while.
(d) Go on reciting, 'Awudhu billahi Minash Shaitan Nirrajeem' (I seek your refuge from the satan).
(e) Avoid reacting immediately to any situation.
(f) Try to come out of the situation.
(g) Repent what you have done before Allah (Istigfar)

(h) Apologise humbly to the person on whom one has vented ones anger, and

Give charity (Sadqa = Voluntary charity).

(iii) DAROOGH (To lie)

Lying is a mental debauchery leading to disgrace. Prophet Mohammed (SAW) reported to have said that false evidence would be the same as to shirk.

(iv) GEEBATH (Backbiting)

Defacing the image of an individual in his absence in spite of his virtues.

Consequences

Geebath has been equated with the act of eating the flesh of one's dead brother.

—*Quran*

Geebath has been described by Prophet Mohammed (PBUH) as worse than fornication.

Prevention

- Look at people's good qualities and admire them.
- Develop a positive opinion about others.

Treatment

- Consider the meaning of the words carefully before uttering them.
- Speak minimally.
- Avoid idleness.

(v) HUB-BE-MAAL AND BUKHL (Love of wealth and miserliness)

- Attachment to wealth and not spending there of when required to do so in the following situations
- When stipulated by the shariat, e.g. Giving of Zakath
- When protecting one's dignity and honour.

Dangers and consequences

- Disgrace awaits such as person in the Akirath.
- He is deprived of the Duas of the poor.

Prevention

- Think of death and the consequences in the grave and the Akirath.
- Keep in mind that Hubb-e-Mall and Bukhl are evils.

Treatment

- Assess one's necessities and budget accordingly.
- Superfluous wealth should be spent in the service of upliftment of the poor.

(vi) HUB-BE-DUNIYA (Love of materialism)

It is getting oneself enslaved to wordly pleasures and for getting of the Akirath.

Consequences

Hub-be-duniya is the root of all evils. He who exhibits no far the sins or crimes he is committing will never care to indulge in causing harm to the others.

Prevention and treatment

- Think about death.
- Meditate on the Akirath.
- Consider oneself a traveler passing through this world.
- Avoid scheming for the unforeseeable future.
- Look at wealth in its proper perspective.

Explanation

Wealth and family do not necessarily constitute Hub-be-duniya. Prophet Mohammed (SAW) states, "Halal wealth is a benefit to pious person."

- It is not against Shariath to save
- It is not against Shariath to possess good items.

(vii) HUB-BE-JAH (Love for fame)

A burning desire to get status and prestige, more than others and to make them submissive.

Consequences

- Hub-be-Jah creates jealousy.
- A bigger danger is that the person will become addicted to it.
- If unchecked, it leads to Takabbur (Arrogance)

Prevention

- Avoid publicity and limelight
- Avoid unnecessary praises and compliments.

Treatment

- Remember that the worldly existence is temporal.
- Remember that even the legendary personalities, such as kings and statesmen, have already passed into historical darkness.

(viii) UJUB (Self-deceit)

When somebody believes that all his achievements are self-attained and not willed by Allah.

Consequences

- This is the first step towards arrogance.
- If a person becomes arrogant, Allah withdraws His grace.

Prevention and treatment

- Acknowledge that all achievements are blessings from Allah and Allah has the power to take them back at any moment.
- Look closely at one's faults and weakness.

(ix) TAKABBUR (Arrogance)

He who is commanded by Takabbur believes that he is the best of all.

Consequences

- It was the arrogance of shaitan that tempted to disobey Allah causing his downfall.
- A Hadith states: "He who has a grain of arrogance in his heart will not enter Jannah." (paradise)
- Takabbur makes people stubborn and naughty.

Prevention

- Acknowledge that Allah alone is perfect in all qualities.
- Correcting at one's own short comings.

(x) RIYAA (Showing-off)

The desire to appear to be good or pious in the eyes of the others thereby acquiring more result and popularity and seeming to be obedient to Allah. The intention is not solely to gain the pleasure of Allah.

Consequences

One's intention in Riyaa is two-fold—Riyaa is considered to be a form of shirk. Instead of seeking Allah's pleasure, a Riyakar (Showoff person) seeks the approval of his fellowmen. In a beautiful tradition, Prophet Mohammed (SAW) had brought out the picture of a show-off person. On the day of Akhirath three persons who are well-known in their domain one of them is greatly charitable; one is highly learned and the third dies for a good cause. The angles present the learned man (Aalim) before Allah for his judgment. Allah asks the learned person to tell about Himself. The learned person presents a report of his learning. He tells Allah that he has learnt several things about Deen and taught the points of Deen to the servants of Allah.

Allah says that the learned person teaching has not

been to please Allah but to get worldly recognition. He tells that the learned person has had his reward on earth itself. He says that the person has no place in Akirath. And the angels push him into the hell.

The Martyr as well as the donor also meet the same fate in the hands of Allah.

The Prophet (PBUH) reported to have said that a deed contaminated by even an atom of Riyaa is not acceptable to Allah.

Prevention and treatment

Two most important things in Islam are intention and motivation. However, good an act may be, if the motivation is not for seeking the pleasure of Allah, the merit of the deed will have no reward.

Voluntary worship (Nafil Ibadat) should be performed in privacy.

(xi) HASAD (Jealousy)

Hasad may be defined as a feeling of a deprived person when he looks at the gifted person. This feeling gives rise to a burning desire that other person's bounties should be ruined.

Dangers and consequences

He who is jealous will incur the displeasure of Allah and even his good deeds will not be recognized or rewarded.

Prophet Mohammed (SAW) warns by saying, "Jealousy destroys good deeds like fire devours wood."

The person who has Hasad loses his contentment and peace of mind. He feels frustrated and it is common knowledge that such a person is thrown into poverty—poverty of ideas, deprivation of power, economic poverty, etc.

Treatment

- Suppress any feeling of jealousy.
- Always speak well of one's opponents.

(xii) KEENAH (Hatred)

When somebody feels hatred towards others for personal reasons and not for the sake of Deen, he is said to have Keenah.

Consequences

- Destroys the internal peace of a person.
- Prophet Mohammed (PBUH) said that both the persons having malice for one another are not forgiven.

Treatment

- Overlook the faults of the person who is the object of one's hatred.
- Be friendly with him.

(B) To encourage the Nafs to do good things. It means that one must acquire all the Akhlaq-e-Hameedah (pious qualities) listed below:

(i) YAQEEN (Conviction)

The muslim should have strong belief in the unity of godhood (Tawheed) the institution of Prophethood (Resalath) and life hereafter (Akhirath). This is also called IMAN. This word is derived from Hebrew language, AMANA, which means grounding oneself.

Acquisition

- Contemplation and meditation will strengthen Tawheed at the intellectual level
- Carrying out the instruction of Allah will complete the process at the practical level.

(ii) IKHLAAS (Sincerity)

The sole intention in one's obedience to Allah, should be to please Him and attain nearness to Him.

Acquisition

- Remove Riyaa
- Concentrate on the quality of deeds and not on the quantity. A Hadith states: "A half mug of corn given in charity by my Sahaba, companions of Prophet Mohammed (PBUH), is nobler than gold equal to mount Uhad given in charity by others." (This is because Sahaba were the embodiment of sincere Muslims).

(iii) SHUKR (Gratitude)

Recognizing that all blessings originate from Allah and repaying to other human beings who have done some good to us is Shukr.

Acquisition

We should recognize, be happy and serve. We should cultivate this habit until it becomes our second nature.

(iv) HILM (Forbearance)

This is a stage higher than sabr. This is one's ability to bring the Nafs under control during difficulties.

Acquisition

- Acquire sabr
- Control anger

(v) SABR (Patience)

It can be described as self-restraint under an extreme provocation, temptation and tiresome tribulations. It is one's ability to control Nafs and continue to be obedient to Allah in the face of difficulties. It is not just a passive bearing of one's burdens but a proactive in doing the following:

(a) Shunning wrong doings during the period of trials of Allah (Aazmaish).
(b) Continue to do righteous deeds in the face of one's problems.

(c) One should not allow the Nafs to dominate the Ruh while one is in difficulties.

Acquisitions

- Understand the true nature of difficulties—look at them as blessings in disguise.
- Remember that Allah will help those who practise Sabr (InnAllaha mass saabireen)

(vi) TAWAKKUL (Trust)

- To have complete faith in Allah on all matters. Tawakkul is based on 3 fundamental principles.
- Marifat (Knowledge of Allah): Complete belief and conviction in the concept of Tawheed with Iqlas and Sidq.
- Haal (Condition): Ease and happiness in every situation. Perfect belief that Allah is in full control of the situation.
- Amaal (Effort): Making necessary efforts according to the Shariat.

Acquisition

Remember that Allah promises bounties and everything in the world happens according to the Mashiat of Allah. Allah is the ultimate decision-maker.

(vii) QANAAT (Contentment)

It is an inner contentment and indifference to everything in Duniya beyond one's necessities.

Acquisition

This can be brought about by understanding the real nature of Duniya.

(viii) ZUHAD (Abstinence)

Giving up a desirable thing in this world in preference to an everlasting thing in the Akirath (world hereafter) Zuhad is not giving-up worldly pleasures.

(ix) ISHQUE (Love of Allah)

Muhabbat (love) means the love felt for a particular object because of the pleasure it provides. Pleasure may be experienced physically (Tabai): When the object influences all the five senses and emotions, giving rise to physical love (Mohabbat Tabai).

- Pleasure may be derived at a mental plane (Aqli), giving rise to love at an intellectual plane (Mohabbat Aqli). Physical love is usually fickle and even immature.
- Intellectual attraction is stable, disciplined and fully controllable.
- The above listed facts do vouchsafe that the object of one's love should be Allah, the Prophet and his Sahabas.

Acquisition

- Recognize Allah's perfections by means of meditation.
- Remove love of everything besides Allah by engaging in constant Zikr.
- Get closure to Allah by submitting completely to His commands by offering Tahajjud (Mid-night prayer).

(x) TAUBAH (Repentance)

The act of turning towards Allah. Taubah is a process that is completed in several stages:

- Possessing knowledge about Halal and Haram.
- Grief (remourse felt at having sinned).
- Resolution-making a mental resolution, not to commit the sin again; uttering words of Istigfar and performing two Rakaths of Salath of Tauba.
- If any harm is done to others, it should be made good.

Acquisition

- Develop fear of Allah and hope.
- Think of the virtues of Tauba and Allah says: "He who makes Tauba after his transgression and reforms, verily Allah turns towards him."—*Quran*
- Be careful in rationalizing the sin. This is the work of Shaitan.

(xi) RAJAA (Hope)

Rajaa means a sensation and a pleasure experienced at the anticipation of something good.

(xii) SIDQ (Honesty)

Sidq is to develop a particular activity sincerely and take it to its logical conclusions. A sidq may be in anyone of the following forms:

Saadiq-ul-aqwaal	—	speaking truth
Saadiq-ul-afall	—	performing duties in conformity with shariat
Saadiq-ul-ahwaal	—	a state of happiness

Acquisition

- Knowledge of what constitutes perfection.
- Close watchfulness of one's deficiencies.
- Repeated convention of these deficiencies.

III. JISMAANI MUJAAHADAH

To control the inclinations of the Nafs, it is necessary that the bodily functions should be reformed and rejuvenated towards the better.

The four training techniques of Mujahadaa Jismani are put to discussion as here under:

- Speaking less,
- Eating less,
- Sleeping less, and
- Associating less with others.

1. Speaking less

Speech can be divided into three classes:

Beneficial	- either to one's Deen or Duniya
Harmful	- to one's Deen as well as Duniya
Worth less	- Laghu—unnecessary and unwarranted speech.

The following Hadith and the verses from Holy Quran stress the importance of limited speech:

Prophet Mohammed (PBUH) has said,
"He who maintains silence has attained salvation."
In another Hadith, the Holy Prophet is reported to have said,
"Do not speak in abundance, other than Zikrullah (Allah's remembrance), for your heart becomes hard."
The Holy Quran describes a successful person as "one who avoids vain talk."

(Quran 23:3)

Acquisition

- Think before you speak and make Istigfar,
- Keep your tongue busy with Zikr, and
- Speak only when it is necessary.

2. Eating less

(i) One should avoid over-eating. But he should eat as much as his stomach takes in, so as to avoid pangs of hunger. Care should be taken that overeating should not lead to health hazards.

(ii) It is always safe and even secure to eat and drink one third of belly and one third of water and one third keeping belly empty. There is a great joy in one's Zikr and Ibadat.

Acquisition

A change in the routine of one's eating is sufficient to

bring about the necessary discipline of the Nafs. Fasting is one of the best exercises. In addition to Ramzan fasting, Nafil (voluntary) fasting is also to be practiced.

Eat according to one's requirements—Eat while hungry and not all the time like a glutton.

3. Sleeping less

The purpose of this exercise is to remove slothfulness of the Nafs. One should try to perform Tahajjud to get more peace of mind. A bright shade of light is reflected in the persons face from the Ibadath at night.

However, sleeping too little may affect the mind. Preference must always be given to Farz Ibadath over Nafil.

Acquisition

Make a habit of sleeping a minimum of six hours a day and a maximum of seven hours.

One's evening schedule should be such as to leave the hours between Isha and Fajr prayers for one's family.

4. Associating less with others

One's association with others should be to match the necessity. Association with others is of three types:

Beneficial—Association commanded by the shariat, to be duty-bound. It is not permissible to terminate this type of association.

Harmful—Association prohibited by Shariat. Termination of this type of association is Wajib.

Neither beneficial nor harmful—Association that cannot be labelled Ibadat, nor does it fall in the category of sinny.

Acquisition

- Draft a daily schedule, allocating time for all one's duty and obligations connected with Deen and Duniya.
- Zikr in solitude is recommended and even endorsed as one finds solace and joy in constant touch with Allah.

Jismani Mujaahadah and Nafsnai Mujaahada are required to discipline the Nafs. The Nafs, in turn, is a force inclining mainly towards evil, and it is attached to the Rooh, suppressing the latter's progress towards seeking Allah's pleasure. To name another impediment in thwarting the Rooh towards Raza-e-Ilahi is Shaitan.

A focus on shaitan and his mechanizations:

Shaitan (Iblis)

Iblis is from among the Jinn, which are special creation of Allah, being created from fire, long before the creation of the human being.

Iblis was an ardent worshipper of Allah. However, he earned the displeasure of Allah after he disobeyed Allah's command to prostrate before Adam. The Angels were obedient and prostrated, but Iblis was adament and arrogant. He tried to justify his arrogance by declaring his creation was far superior to that of Adam. This arrogance earned him the wrath of Allah. Iblis refused to make Tauba seal his fate. This is precisely the reason for calling him Shaitan (one who opposes).

The Human being had been already warned and this warning is repeated in the Quran and the Ahadith is about the evil designs of shaitan. Shaitan had taken an oath to attack human beings from all sides and divert them from the straight moral path. Shaitan cannot rest in peace unless he makes every possible attack on the Nafs of the human being. No one is immune to the shaitan's cunning attacks. At no point of time he spares human beings. For shaitan no place is too remote to attack or to reveal his evil scheming.

Repelling Shaitan

No doubt, Allah has created man weak, but has armed him with powerful weapons. Allah has provided different methods of defending oneself from Shaitan.

Three such weapons are:

- Reciting Tawooz (I seek refuge in Allah from the pangs of Shaitan).

- Engaging in Zikrullah constant communication with Allah.

OTHER METHODS OF TASAWUF

In the previous pages, an attempt has been made to draw on the knowledge provided by Islamic mystics to train the human beings as well as organizational members so that they can be brought back to the original nature of man, i.e. his craving for seeking the pleasure of God. In the following pages the researcher describes and discusses some such training programmes for the organizations.

The following are some such schedules:

TAZKIYA-E-QALB (Cleansing of the heart)

Qalb stands for heart. In Sufi terminology this is referred to as the spiritual heart. It is the seat of beatific vision. It is also considered as the gate of divine love and for others, it is the battle ground of two warring armies,: those of Nafs and Rooh. Cleansing of the Qalb is a pre-requisite for spiritual growth of a human being so that he can receive divine love.

Sufis divide the progress of their Qalb towards Allah into seven stages which are called the spiritual excellences (Lata-if—e-Qalbi). At each stage the qalb gets new characteristics, develops new qualities and acquires new properties.

The following are the seven stages:

1. Watching the heart (Wuquf-e-Qalbi)
2. Watching the number (Wuquf-e-Adadi)
3. Watching the time (Wuquf-e-Zamani)
4. Remembrance (Yad-dasht)
5. Retirement (Baz-gasht)
6. Carefulness (Nigah-dasht)
7. Forgetfulness (Khud-gudhast)

The above stages signify the movement of the soul towards attainment of the object of the Qalb's love and admiration. This schedule was worked out to train the disciples of Sufi school of thought. The same can be utilised by Muslim as well as non-muslim organizations to train their members. Some of these seven stages of spiritual development will be discussed in the following pages.

In Islamic theory of motivation it was proved based on Quran and Hadith the following:

- Allah in His own immutable state attribute and being, without altering His individuality, manifests Himself through His attribute of light or in the form of phenomenal objects including human beings. The essence of human beings subsists in the knowledge of God and hence it is that the divine aspect has come to be associated with human beings.
- As man is endowed with this divine sparkle he will have to strive to keep his knowledge always before his mind's eye. In other words, he should be able to feel the presence of Allah every moment. This will help him to please his Creator by minding his work as if it is worship. To feel the presence of Allah, it is binding that man should be watchful of his heart. The heart begins to concentrate its attention upon itself. At this stage, the heart starts feeling its own existence. The seeker makes a start by repeating some Zikr, taught to him by the Prophet.
- The second stage gains prominence with the advanced practice of repeating the names of Allah, according to a fixed number.
- The third stage is marked with the seeker's rising above time. This conception of Allah trespasses time and the seeker is taken on his flights of imagination and mental vision. This will take him high and lead him above the limitations of conceiving things in time.
- When he once rises, above his natural or instinct wise weaknesses of human nature, he becomes eligible to receive the vision of Allah.

- The fourth stage is the remembrance of Allah and realizing His reality in one's heart. This is realization and not Zikr. When the seeker begins to realize Allah's attributes in his heart, he must delink himself with worldly things. At this stage, he hears from none but Him. He sees none but Him. He touches nothing but reality and this is the fifth stage.
- When he attains the sixth stage, he should be careful in preserving this state of affairs. He must make an effort to perpetuate this condition.
- After he has sufficiently persevered in his efforts, he is to forget and should not love anything other than Allah. This forgetfulness of everything besides Him is a symbol of perpetual bliss.
- From the above it should not be construed that man should give-up all worldly activities. Since he is vicegerent of Allah, he should perform all the duties and discharge all his responsibilities towards himself, his family members, his society, his organization and, in short, to the world at large as Khalifa of Allah.

TAKHLIYA-E-SIRR (Emptying of the sirr)

Sirr is the third faculty located in the middle of the chest. Emptying of the Sirr is basically to focus on God's names and attributes. This is also called Zikr. It diverts one's attention from the mundane aspects by fixing it on the spiritual realm. This emptying leads to the negation of ego-centred human propensities.

TAJLIYA-E-ROOH (Illumination of the spirit)

Rooh is an immortal entity. It is a soul-spark. Tajliya-e-Rooh means filling the spirit with ardent love of God, which can be generated through prayer (Ibadat).

The Doctrine of Peak Experience

This is also known as ecstasy or rapture. The seeker should deepen his devotion while praying to reach the Nadir (maximum) of his spiritual experience. This is based on the

Hadith in which Prophet Mohammed (PBUH) reported to have said, "you should pray to God as if you see Him and if you cannot see Him, you should visualize that He sees you." It is on the definition of Ihsan that many sufis have built their theory of devotion. Some sufis have taken the doctrine of Nadir experience to its logical conclusion by prescribing Zikr and meditation, devotional songs, and light music as the road to attain such as ecstasy.

6

Summary and Conclusion

The need for the study has stemmed from the fact that the claim of the Western theories of motivation that they are universally applicable and for all times to come has proved to be incorrect. This has necessitated the researcher to propound the universally applicable theory, based on divine guidance.

The study was undertaken mainly to propose an Islamic theory of motivation and to articulate the process of self-purification and suggest training programmes to the organizations to motivate their employees on proper lines.

This study has departed from the traditional research methodology of empirical investigation. Islam accepts an empirical research and its findings as long as they are not repugnant to the revealed knowledge. Islam insists that the seraphic revelation has to be accepted as the source of absolute knowledge. This revelation—not just to Muslims but to the entire mankind, is passed on through Prophet Mohammed (PBUH) in two forms:

The Holy Quran—the immutable word of Allah and Hadith—the inspired sayings and doings of Prophet Mohammed (PBUH)

This study has drawn information extensively from the Holy Quran and the Hadith. Islamic jurisprudence and

Islamic mysticism have been consulted to articulate the Islamic Theory of Motivation.

In Chapter III, a review of various Western Theories of Motivation and an Indian Theory of Motivation are presented in addition to the Islamic Critique of these theories to strengthen the relevance and factual truth of the theme of the study.

In Chapter IV, the Islamic Theory of Motivation has been propounded. Questions such as how the world was created; what the stuff with which it is made of, how the human being was created and what the essence that he posses have been placed on the verbal dais of a detailed discussion. Islam has placed mankind on the ladder of supremacy over the other creatures. Human beings are the vicegerents of All merciful Allah and the cordial ties binding man and the Creator are but the cross of love and affection, faith and devotion. Islam advocates self-transcendence as the chief goal of human life.

The Islamic Theory of Motivation should not be misunderstood as to mean that human effort is not needed for self-transcendence. Man's strivings tinged with the benevolence of All Graceful Allah will land man very near to Allah, the Benefactor of humanity.

For realizing the ultimate goal of human beings, i.e. seeking the pleasure of God, different cultural intervening strategies suggested and supplemented by theologists and mystics find place in Chapter V.

Muslim theologists and Sufis have endorsed the process of purification of self (Tazkiya-e-Nafs) as the sharpening-store to mould the character of human beings. They classify nafs into three categories, namely,

Nafsul-Ammara,
Nafsul-Lawwama, and
Nafsul-Muthmainna.

The first stage of development of self is called Nafsul-Ammara (Evil consciousness). This is the stage of nafs which is prone to evil. Nafsul-Lawwama (Balance consciousness) is the second stage on the spiral staircase of development. At this stage, the message of Allah is introduced to human consciousness. It is only an acquaintance; just a small step that will end up as a giant leap.

A mere grasping of Shariat (Divine Law) is not strong enough to ensure the total eradication of evil. Occasionally, temptations do get an upper hand. Like the villain and the hero. But on the whole, the virtuous propensities dominate the evil inclinations. The consciousness transforms into a self-introspective and critical of one's motives and deeds. It is a stage of discrimination between the right and wrong. The Moral-self becomes distinguished from the brutual physical-self. From mere awareness, it progresses into a discriminating, rejecting and selecting consciousness.

As along as nafs continues to obey the shariah so long it continues to enjoy the higher strata christened as Nafsul Muthmainna, the ultimate in the processes of spiritual development. Like a brave warrior it achieves this stage by constant struggle for doing good. The boat of Nafs anchors on the shores of this highest stage by sailing across with the rudders of faith and good deeds. The mind will experience solace and confidence in its Creator. It is with regard to this nafs that the Quran says:

> "Allah is well pleased with them and they are well pleased with Him."
>
> *(Quran 98:8)*

In another place the Quran says:

> "O tranquil soul! Return to your Lord well pleased (with Him) well pleasing (Him)."
>
> *(Quran: 27-18)*

It is a creditable condition of total submission to its Master. It is further conditioned by the complete satisfaction of mind which is has broken the shackles of cares of the lower animal instincts and which remains distinctly the devoid of chaos and confusion; pains and problems.

For graduating Nafsul-Ammara to Nafsul-Muthmainna, the theologists lay stress on the exact and well-structured belief system and virtuous life. The Sufis approach to Tazkiye-Nafs can be categories as two types of training programmes namely,

Mujahada (Disciplining the Nafs), and
Taskiya-e-Qalb (cleansing of the heart)

There are two types of Mujahada;

Nafsani-Mujahada (controlling the Nafs), and
Jismani-Mujahada (controlling the physiological needs).

Nafsani-Mujahada advocates the shirking of Akhlaaq-e-Razeelah (debasing qualities). The seeker is cleverly trained to drive away anger, avarice, back biting, lying, love of wealth, love of material, love for fame, self-deceit, arrogance, showing off, jealousy and hatred like the west wind that forces the dry and dead leaves get scattered.

Nafsani Mujahada aims at possessing the fabulous jewel box Akhalaaq-e-Hameedah (pious qualities) such as sincerity, gratitude, forbearance, patience, trust in Allah, contentment, abstinence, love of Allah, repentance, hope and honesty.

The sugar coated pills of advice that—Mujahada-Jismani is grossly interested in administering are: (a) speaking less, (b) eating less, (c) sleeping less, and (d) associating less with others.

According to Sufis the human heart (Qalb) is the seat of the idea of Allah. It has no association with the human organism called heart. It is a spiritual faculty. Sufis consider it as a kind of mirror that reflects the reality of Allah. It is through this Qalb that human beings come into contact with their Creator. Sufis call the process of development of Qalb towards infinity as Tazkiya-e-Qalb.

The following is the list of seven key stages of Tazkiya-e-Qalb (purificaqtion of heart).

Watching the heart (Wuquf-e-Qalbi),
Watching the number (Wuquf-e-Adadi),
Watching the time (Wuquf-e-Zamani),
Remembrance (Yad-dasht),
Retirement (Baz-gasht),
Carefulness (Nigah-dasht), and
Forgetfulness (Khud-gudhast).

Glossary

Abd	:	A Worshipper.
Adl	:	Justice, equilibrium, and equity. A fundamental value governing all social behaviours forming the basis of all social dealings and legal frameworks.
Akhirah	:	Hereafter.
Ahadith	:	Plural of Hadeeth.
Allah	:	Creator of Universe and Sustainer of all. Supreme Being. God.
Amale Salih	:	Good deeds.
Arsh	:	The Throne (of Allah).
Ayat	:	A section of the text of the Quran referred to as a "verse." It literally means sign, indication or message.
Caliph	:	Khalifah: The leader of the Muslim Ummah.
Dhiya	:	Waste.
Deen	:	Religion, a way of life. Used to refer to Islam and the way of life it ordains.
Dua	:	Supplication to Allah. Invocation.
Dunya	:	World/Earth.
Falah	:	Success (in life hereafter).
Fardh	:	Some thing which is obligatory. Such as five times prayer daily.
Fiqh	:	Jurisprudence.
Hadith	:	Narrations and reports of the deeds and sayings of the Holy Prophet (Sal).
Haj	:	Pilgrimage during the month of Dul Haj to Makkah where the Kaba, the House of Allah, is located.
Halal	:	Anything permitted by the Shariah (Islamic

		Law). Lawful.
Haqq	:	Right. Truth.
Haram	:	Anything prohibited by the Shariah (Islamic Law). Unlawful.
Hidayah	:	Divine guidance.
Hikmah	:	One's ability to put knowledge (ilm) into practice.
Hilm	:	Forbearance.
Ibadah	:	Worship.
Ijtihad	:	Islamic method of arriving decision on opinions based on guiding principle when faced with new situation.
Ijma	:	Consensus of Opinion.
Ilm	:	Knowledge.
Iman	:	Belief in the article of faith enunciated in the Quran and the Sunnah.
Insha Allah	:	God willing.
Islam	:	To submit and offer peace. The religion of all the Prophets of Allah confirmed finally by the mission of the Prophet Mohamed (Sal).
Istislah	:	Public interest.
Jannah	:	Paradise. Heaven.
Jahannam	:	Hell
Jihad	:	To struggle. "Any earnest striving in the way of Allah, involving either personal effort, material resources, or arms for righteousness and against evil, wrongdoing and oppression."
Jinn	:	Invisible beings constituting a whole race like mankind.
Kabah	:	A cube-shaped building built by the Prophets Ibrahim and Ismail (Als).
Khalifah	:	Caliph, Vicegerent, Ruler. "The word Khalifah was used after the death of the Prophet Mohamed (Sal) to refer to his successors, Abu Bakr (Ral), Umar (Ral), Uthman (Ral) and Ali (Ral).
Kufr	:	Covering, hiding or being ungrateful. In Islam, it means rejecting any or all articles of faith.

Madinah : The city in Arabia where the Prophet Mohammed (Sal) is buried.
Makkah/ Mecca : The city in Arabia where the holy Kabah is situated.
Marifat : Spiritual Realisation (of Allah).
Mumin : One who has iman.
Muslim : Believers in one God and the Prophet Mohamed (Sal) . One who submits to the Will of God.
Nafs : Self.
Nafil : Non-Obligatory, Optional.
Noor : Light, Effulgence.
PBUH : Peace be upon him.
Qiblah : Kiblah, The direction (toward the Kabah in Makkah) all Muslims must face when performing prayer from any given point on earth.
Quran : The final book or revelation from Allah to mankind, revealed to the Prophet Mohamed (Sal) over a span of 23 years.
Qiyaamah : The Day of Judgment.
Ral : Razhiallahu anhu (male) Razhiallahu anha (female) May Allah pleased with him or her.
Rasulullah : Messenger of Allah—Prophet Mohamed (Sal).
Sabr : Observing patience.
Sahaba : Companions of the Prophet Mohamed (Sal) during his life.
Sal : Abbreviated words of honour and salutations attached to the name of the Holy Prophet.
Mohamed (Sal) : Meaning May Allah send blessings and salutations on him.
Swt : Subhanahu Ta'ala.
Shariah : A path. It is used to mean Islam's legal system that Muslims abide by.
Shirk : Setting up partners with the Allah.
Sunnah : A tradition or practice. The body of traditions and practices of the Prophet (Sal); also includes his words, actions, or what has been approved by him.
Sufi : A Mystic.

Taqwa	: Piety-fear of Consciousness of Allah.
Tawhid/ Tauheed	: The belief in the uniqueness of Allah.
Tajalli	: Radiance.
Tasawwuff	: Sufi-ism.
Tawooz	: I seek protection from the pangs of shaitan.
Ummah	: Refers to the community of believers worldwide, irrespective of colour, race, language, nationality or boundaries. The universal body of Muslims as a single community.
Uhad	: A mountain in Madeena.
Wahy	: Revelation from Allah.
Wajib	: Obligatory.
Zakah	: Poor due. The amount, at least 2.5 percent payable annually by a Muslim on his net savings as a part of his religious obligation, mainly for the benefit of the poor and the needy.
Zikrullah	: Remembrance of Allah.
Zulm	: Tyranny. A comprehensive term used to refer to all forms of inequity, injustice exploitation, oppression, and wrongdoing, whereby a person either deprives others of their rights or does not fulfil his obligations toward them.

Bibliography

Azam, M.A., 1979, "Leadership": Islamic Foundation Bangladesh, Dacca.

Abdul Hakim, Khalifa, 1987, "The Prophet and His Message", Institute of Islamic Culture, Pakistan.

Akbar Mohideen, M., 2005, "Leadership Style and Shura System in Islamic Culture", a formulative study of traits and moral bases of leaders. Unpublished Ph.D. Thesis, University of Madras, Chennai.

Adorno, T.W., Frenkel-Brunswick, E., Levinson, D.J, and Sanford, R.N., 1950, "The Authoritarian Personality", Herper, New York.

Al-Buraey, Muhammad, 1985, "Management and Administration in Islam", Kegan Paul Interntional Ltd., UK.

Andrae, T., 1936, "Mohammed: The Man and his Faith", George Allen and Unwin Ltd.

Allport, G.W. and Ross, J.M., 1967, "Personal Religious Orientation and Prejudice", *Journal of Personality and Social Psychology*.

Alderfer, C.P., 1969, "An Empirical Test of a new theory of human needs, Organizational Behaviour and Human Performance."

Arnold, H.J., 1976, "Effects of Performance Feedback and Extrinsic Reward upon High Intrinsic Motivation", Organizational Behaviour and Human Performance.

Bangash Zafar, 2000, "The Concept of Leader and Leadership in Islam", The Institute of Contemporary Islamic Thought, London.

Barnard Chester, 1968, "The functions of the Executive", Harvard University Press, Cambridge, Mass.

Beekun, Rafik and Jamal Badawi, 1999, "Leadership an Islamic Perspective", Amana Publications, Maryland, USA.

Bond, M.H. and K.K. Hwang, 1986, "The Social Psychology of Chinese People", Hong Kong: Oxford University Press.

Berger, P., Assessment of Managers—An International Comparison, New York Free Press.

Becker Howard, 1941, "Supreme Values and the Sociologist", *American Sociological Review.*

Bennis, Warren G., 1966, "Changing Organisations", Tata McGraw Hill Publishing Company, New Delhi.

Bass, B.M. and P.C. Burger, 1979, "Assessment of Managers": An International Comparison, New York: Free Press.

Burger, P. and Doktor, R., 1976, "Self-Perception attitudes among Managers from different Countries", *Management International Review.*

Chakraborthy, S.K., 1980, "Management Stylistics in India: The case for Countervailing Ethoes", *Decision.*

Cambell, D.I., 1956, "Leadership and its effect upon the group", Columbus: Ohio State University, Bureau of Business Research.

Calder, B.J. and Staw, B.M., 1975, "Study Perception of Intrinsic and Extrinsic Motivation", *Journal of Personality and Social Psychology.*

Catwright, D. and Zender, A., eds. 1960, "Group Dynamics: Research and Theory", 2nd ed., Evanston, III: Row, Peterson.

Carlyle, T., 1907, "Heroes and Hero Worship", Boston: Adams (first published 1841).

Chaudhari, *et al.*, 1982, "Patterns of Diversification in Larger Indian Enterprises", *Vikalpa.*

Connr Patrick, E. and Becker Boris, W., 1974, "Values and Comparative Organizational Research", Proceedings of the Academy of Management.

Davis, K., 1980, "Human Behaviour at Work", Organizational Behaviour, Tata McGraw Hill Publishing Co. Ltd., New Delhi.

David, J. Chrrington: 1994, "Organizational Behaviour", Allyn and Bacon, Boston.

Deci, E.L., 1975, "Intrinsic Motivation", Newyork: Plenum.

Dwivedi, R.S., 1984, "A Study of Some Behavioural Determinants of Organizational Performance in Public Enterprises", *Lok Udyog*.

De N., 1974, "Conditions for Work Culture", *Indian Journal of Industrial Relations*.

Dhingra, O.P. and Pathak, V.K., 1972, "Professional Background of the Indian Personnel Manager", *PACT*.

Dwivedi, R.S., 1970, "The Relative Importance of Personality Traits Among Indian Managers", *Indian Management*.

Ervin Laszlo, 1973, "A System Philosophy of Human Values, Behavioural Science."

Etizioni, Amitai, 1961, "Complex Organizations", New York: Holt, Rinehart & Winston.

Festinger, L., 1954, "A Theory of Social Comparison processes", *Human Relations*.

Fromm, E., 1965, "The Heart of Man: Its Genius for Good and Evil", London: Routiedge and Kegan Paul Ltd.

Gibb, C.A., 1954, "Leadership in Gardner Lindzey", ed., Handbook of Social Psychology, Cambridge, Mass: Addition-Wesley.

Ghalib Hussain, Mohammed, 1991, "Personal Values, Personality and Management Behaviour"—A Study based on Selected Organizations, unpublished Ph.D. thesis Submitted to the University of Madras, Chennai.

Gellerman, S.W., 1968, "Management by Motivation", American Management Association, New York.

Gerigaliunas, B.S. and Herzberg, F., 1971, "Relevency in the test of Motivation Hygiene Theory", *Jounal of Applied Psychology*.

Ganesh, S.R., "Research in Organizational Behaviour in India 1970-79: A Critique", Indian Institute of Management, Ahmedabad, India, August 1981.

Heresy, P. and K.H. Blanchard, 1982, "Management of Organizational Behaviour", Utilizing Human Resources, Englewood Cliffs, NJ: Prentice-Hall.

Hiriyann, M., 1956, "Essentials of Indian Philosophy", London: George Allen and Unwin.

Hilliard, A.L., 1950, "The Forms of Value", Columbia University Press, New York.

Husein Haykal, 1993, "The Life of Muhammed: English Translation by Ismail Raji Al-Faruqi, Kulalumpur.

Hofstede, G., 1980, "Culture's Consequences: International Differences in Work-related Values", Beverly Hills, CA: Sage.

Herzberg, F. Mausner, B. and Syndermen, 1959, "The Motivation to Work", Newyork: John Wiley.

Izraeli, D., 1988, "Ethical Beliefs and Behaviour among Managers", A Cross-cultural Perspective", *Journal of Business Ethics*.

Jawdal Sa'eed, 1983, Work a Skill and a Will, Damascus.

Jabnoun, Naceur, 2001, "Islam and Management", International Islamic Publishing House, Riyadh, Saudi Arabia.

Kalim, Siddiqui, 1998, "Political Dimensions of the Seerah": The Institute of Contemporary Islamic Thought, London.

Kegan, R., 1982, "The Evolving Self: Problem and Process in Human Development", Cambridge M.A.: Harvard University Press.

Koontz, Harold, and O'Donnell, Cyril, 1972, "Principles of Management": An analysis of Managerial Functions", McGraw Hill Book Company Inc., Tokyo.

Kluckhohn, C., 1951, "Values and Value Orientations in the theory of Action", Toward a General Theory of Action, Cambridge Harvard University Press.

Korman, A.K., Greenhans, J.H. and Badin, I.J., 1977, "Personal Attitudes and Motivation", *Annual Review of Psychology*.

Lall, 1982, "The Emergence of Third World Multinationals", Indian Joint Ventures Overseas, *World Development*.

Lawler, E.E., 1973, "Motivation in Work Organizations", Monterg, Call Brooks Cole Publishing Co.

Lawler, E.E. and Porter, L.W., 1976, "The Effect of Performance on Job Satisfaction", London: The Macmillan Press Ltd.

Locke, E.A., 1968, "Towards a Theory of Task Motivation and Incentives", *Organizational Behaviour and Human Performance.*

Maudoodi, Sayyid Abul A'la, 2000, "Towards Understanding Islam", *Markazi,* Maktaba Islami Publishers, New Delhi.

Muhammed Yousuf Khandhelwi, 1985, "The Lives of Sahaba", (An English Translation of "Hayathus Sahaba" Originally in Arabic, Idara-e-Isha'at-e-Diniyat (P) Ltd., New Delhi.

Maslow, A.H., 1964, "Religious, Values and Peak-experiences." Columbus, Ohio: Phio State University Press.

Maslow, A.H., 1954, "New Knowledge in Human Values", New York: Harper and Row.

Maslow, A.H., 1954, "Motivation and Personality", Newyork: Herper.

McDougall, William, 1918, "An Introduction to Social Psychology", Boston: John W. Luce and Co.

McClelland, D.C., 1953, "The achievement motive", Newyork: Appleton-Century Crofts.

McClelland, D.C., 1976, "Power is the Great Motivator", *Harvard Business Review.*

Mirza, S. Saiyadain, 1976, "Job Enrichment: Prospects and Problems", Indian Institute of Management, Ahmedabad.

Maheshwari, 1980, "Decision Styles and Organisational Effectiveness", New Delhi: Vikas Publishing House.

Maudoodi, Sayyid, Abu A'la, 1991, "The Islamic Movement: Dynamics of Values, Power and Change", The Islamic Foundation, U.K.

Maslow, A.H., 1954, "Motivation and Personality", New York: Harper.

McClellend, D.C., 1969, "That Urge to Achieve Readings in Management", Ohio: South Western Publishing Coopany.

McGregor, D., 1960, "The Human side of Enterprise", Tata McGraw Hill Publishing Co., Ltd.

Moten, Rashid, A., 1989, "Islamization of Knowledge:

Methodology of Research in Political Science", *The American Journal of Islamic Social Sciences.*

Mohammed Yusuf Islahi, 2000, "Etiquette of Life in Islam", Markazi Maktaba Islami Publishers, New Delhi.

Muqim Mohammed, 1994, "Research Methodology in Islamic Perspective", Institute of Objective Studues, New Delhi.

Patrick, R. Penland, 1974, "Group Dynamics and Individual Development", New York: Dekker.

Posner, B. and W. Schmidt, 1993, "Value Congruence and Differences between the Interplay of Personal and Organisational Value Systems", *Journal of Business Ethics.*

Porter, L.W., 1961, "A Study of Perceived Need Satisfaction in Bottom and Middle Management Jobs", *Journal of Applied Psychology,* 45(1).

Qutab, Muhummad, 1982, "Islam: The Misunderstood Religion", *Markazi Maktaba Islami,* New Delhi.

Quradawi, Y.A., 1960, "The Lawful and Prohibited in Islam", Hindustan Publications.

Robert, R. Blake and Jane, S. Mouton, 1964, "The Managerial Grid", Houston, Tex.: Gulf Publishing Company.

Ritz, G., 1984, "Sociological Theory", New York: Alfred Knopf.

Rosenberg, M., 1957, "Occupations and Values", The Free Press, Glencoe.

Roy, S. and Dhawan, S.K., 1984, "Indian Managers and Their Values", *Indian Journal of Industrial Relations.*

Safi, Louay, 1995, "Leadership and Subordination: An Islamic Perspective", *The American Journal of Islamic Social Sciences,* Volume 12.

Stephen, P. Robbins, 2001, "Organizational Behaviour", Prentice-Hall Inc., New Jersey, U.S.A.

Singh, J.P., 1990, "Managerial Culture and Work-related Values in India", *Organizational Studies.*

Singh, J.P., 1990, "Managerial Culture and Work Related Values in India", *Organizational Studies,* pp. 75-101.

Staw, B.M., 1977, "Motivation in Organizations: Towards Synthesis and Redirection", New Directions in Organizational Behaviour.

Taha Jabir-al-Alwani, 1993, "Source Methodology in Islamic Jurisprudence", English Edn. By Yusuf Talal Delorenzo and Anas, S.-al-Shaikh-Ali, International Institute of Islamic Thought, USA.

Vroom, V.H., 1964, "Work and Motivation", New York: John Wiley and Sons.

Watt, M.W., 1972, "Muhammed: Prophet and Statesman", Oxford University Press, London.

White, R.W., 1959, "Motivation Revisited: The Concept of Competence", *Psychological Review*.

Yahya, Abu Zakaria, 1987, "Riyadh-us-Salaheen", Arabic-English, Kitab Bhavan, New Delhi.

Index